Half a Dialogue…

One Catholic's Reply to Pope Francis' Invitation to Discuss the Encyclical Laudato Si'

by Diane C. Harris

<u>**Author's Note:**</u> Given the need to respond to the Encyclical on a timely basis, and the inclusion of serious subject matter and concerns separate from faith and morals, no Imprimatur or statement of Nihil Obstat was sought, nor was any refused.

Nevertheless, for the sake of not being a stumbling block to the reader, I affirm my belief in all that the Catholic Church teaches and, to the best of my knowledge and ability, I state that nothing I have written herein contains anything which contradicts the teachings of the Catholic Church.

<u>Act of Faith</u>

O my God, I firmly believe
that You are one God in three Divine Persons,
Father, Son, and Holy Spirit.
I believe that Your Divine Son became man
and died for our sins and that He will come
to judge the living and the dead.
I believe these and all the truths
which the Holy Catholic Church teaches
because You have revealed them
Who are eternal truth and wisdom,
Who can neither deceive nor be deceived.
In this faith I intend to live and die. Amen.

Source: website of United States Conference of Catholic Bishops:
www.USCCB.org

ISBN: 978-0-9968255-0-4
First Printing, December 2015
Second Printing, March 2016

A Hypot[SM] Publication
www.HypotPublishing.com
a division of Hypotenuse Enterprises, Inc.
1545 East Avenue, Rochester, NY 14610
Hypot[SM] and Hypotenuse[SM] are registered service marks
of Hypotenuse Enterprises, Inc.

ACKNOWLEDGEMENTS

Thank God for God!
Father, Son and Holy Spirit.

Gratitude is extended to His Holiness, Pope Francis,
Who has graciously invited an unprecedented level of
dialogue, discussion and debate in response to
his Encyclical, Laudato Si'.

I particularly offer appreciation to those with whom
I have shared the studying of Sacred Scripture,
for the teachers who have challenged me,
the friends who have encouraged me,
and all who have counseled me,
whether in formal situations or over a cup of coffee.

It is impossible to try to name all the individuals
who deserve special mention; surely some
would be omitted inadvertently. However, in the direct effort
of production of **"Half a Dialogue"** there are three people
who deserve particular recognition:

>> Philip C. L. Gray, JCL, is President of The St. Joseph Foundation, which
is dedicated to uphold Catholic Truth and defend Catholic Rights.
His tireless devotion to righteousness and
his impeccability as a resource of courage and virtue
have been of inestimable support and encouragement to me.

>> Barbara Merla, my Executive Assistant, has worked with me
every step of the way on this project. Her persistence and stamina
are particularly noteworthy. Her candor and humor have been essential.
And she never lost sight of the 'vision.'

>> Milton Lederman, Ph.D. acted as editor, proof-reader, grammarian
and punster par excellence!
Any errors which survived his edit were most likely
added by me after the edit.
Any puns which survived were most likely
added by Dr. Lederman when I wasn't looking.

DEDICATION PRAYER

This work is dedicated to the Oneness of the Catholic Church, praying that everything herein will lead to greater unity in the Body of Christ so that, in the oneness of faith, nothing divides us. The four "marks" of the Church (one, holy, catholic and apostolic) are not possessed by the Church of herself; it is Christ, through the Holy Spirit, Who makes His Church One. He prayed for Unity the night before He died, when He asked the Father:

(John 17:17-23): "Sanctify them in the truth; Thy word is truth. As Thou didst send Me into the world, so I have sent them into the world. And for their sake I consecrate Myself, that they also may be consecrated in truth. I do not pray for these only, but also for those who believe in Me through their word, that they may all be one; even as Thou, Father, art in Me, and I in Thee, that they also may be in Us, so that the world may believe that Thou hast sent Me. The glory which Thou hast given Me I have given to them, that they may be one even as We are one, I in them and Thou in Me, that they may become perfectly one, so that the world may know that Thou hast sent Me and hast loved them even as Thou hast loved Me."

This single passage illustrates how inseparable are Truth and Oneness. In some vital sense, Truth may be seen as the seamless garment of Oneness. How alienating from God, and how divisive in a community, is any departure from Truth. While what first compelled me to read and comment on Laudato Si' was commitment to scientific truth, Truth Himself has no exceptions. I was soon drawn deeper into Laudato Si'. To the best of my ability, I have only written what I believe to be truth, and I pray that Truth will overcome any temptation to division among the Faithful.

I regret if, for lack of clarity or lack of gentleness, any materials are presented in an offensive or divisive manner, for my intent has been quite the opposite. Let us pray that the Holy Father's invitation to dialogue will bear much fruit.

Diane C. Harris

TABLE OF CONTENTS

FOREWORD

Pope Francis' Encyclical, Laudato Si', first caught my attention in February, 2015, when it was still in draft, and I realized he had embraced the current 'Global Warming' / 'Climate Change' allegations fully. I began to think of Pope Urban VIII's assertion of a geocentric theory of the universe, obviously without proof. In a wider sense, Laudato Si' looms as being, in its own time, 'geocentric' as well, focused as it is on the planet. I cringe at the thought, since 'global warming' also is unproved, that such an Encyclical could cause the Catholic Church, which should be a bastion of Truth on every level, to receive criticism and ridicule.

Nine months before learning of the impending Encyclical, I had written an opinion piece for a local newspaper criticizing the claims of 'global warming' (See Appendix A). My opinion has not changed, but it would be less than honest not to acknowledge, right here in the Foreword, that I have asserted and continue to assert that 'global warming' (and its follow-on designation of 'climate change,' trying to cover the embarrassment of global cooling data), is still unproved, although not necessarily untrue. The point is that we simply do not know if it is true or not, for a number of reasons, some of which are summarized in that opinion essay. Intellectual honesty does not entitle us to proceed as if what is either unproved or disproved is therefore true, or to yield to any interpretation beyond adequate data.

A key question

It is a reasonable question to ask: "What would be the harm in 'acting as if' global warming and climate change were true? The answer is that a government, which has an inherent fiduciary duty to its citizens, or any influential organization enjoying a public trust, is irresponsible as a public steward when it asserts something is true, funds it with extensive monetary resources and human energy, distracts from more important needs and priorities, all based on what 'might or might not' be true. It redirects action from where real attention is needed, forces choices that should not be required to be made on a speculative basis and erodes trust. A number of those choices would directly take aid from the poor, whom Pope Francis has often recognized as a prime concern. And all that investment might not even be effective, but just divert resources from more important uses.

Personal Reluctance

From start to finish, this has not been a project I have wanted to undertake. Although I have had a free will choice whether or not to do so, I have not had a conscience choice. I have felt a strong call to respond, for the sake of Truth. As a scientist by education and training, I have likewise felt an obligation to reply to pseudo-scientific allegations based on the fallacy of 'consensus,' which promote 'global warming' and 'climate change' as if 'proven.' Consensus is no respecter of Truth. If it were, we would not have the permissive social environment in which we all live today, impacting souls even more than any alleged theoretical changes in the physical, earthly environment might do.

More than any other organization, the Catholic Church should be making that point in Truth. Error, misunderstanding, and poor communication become even more problematic when the Church, founded by Jesus Christ, Truth Himself, calls for worldwide action on something which may not even be true.

It is not possible to dismiss (or to accept) the Encyclical Laudato Si' without fully examining the text. And, because of the office Pope Francis holds, considering what he has written in serious detail, such study would be merited just because he is the Vicar of Christ. Hence, it was for these reasons, I felt compelled to study Laudato Si' fully, and to do so carefully.

Not being aware of what I would find in the Encyclical, I nevertheless approached the task with a general wariness about any alignment with those who have promulgated the 'global warming' consensus, or popularized it as being a crisis.

I also have an orientation, from my own background in science and business and, to some extent, in appreciation for philosophy (especially logic), about the riskiness of building an intellectual temple upon the shaky ground of the unproven and still disputed. Half-truth is no truth at all. I credit 16 years with Dominican teachers for their 'Veritas' emphasis.

Dear Pope Francis?

My first thought was not to wait for the Encyclical, but rather to write to Pope Francis directly and express concern before publication of Laudato Si'. Actually, I did write that letter, revised it several times, but did not send it. Partly I held back because the global-warming issue had morphed into other concerns and the letter format had become unwieldy. Many of those related concerns did surface in the Encyclical, and they flowed into these writings; e.g. Pantheism, syncretism, subsidiarity, collectivism and confusion with the global-sustainability agenda.

I also tried to revise that intended letter to Pope Francis into a journal article but, as the weeks ticked by and publication of the Encyclical drew closer (with some of that content leaked in the popular press, spreading rapidly beyond the original expectation) it became necessary to wait for the actual publication of Laudato Si'.

Environmentalism: startling subject for an encyclical

About a decade ago, I knew a quite 'liberal' pastor (and his committees) who made recommendations for parish Lenten sacrifices, which should have been prayer, fasting and almsgiving. Instead, they proposed recycling and cleaning up the environment. I remember others in that parish also being outraged at shortchanging God in order to substitute what is already a natural expectation, to keep clean what God has given us, and which benefits our own personal environment, but hardly seems of any significant spiritual sacrifice or merit. (It had all been a bit reminiscent of choosing to diet or exercise for Lent! Would that be for God or for ourselves?)

Yet, as outrageous as such proposed 'environmental sacrifice' had seemed previously, it would turn out to be not all that far away from what I would eventually read in Laudato Si'. That Lenten memory also impelled the need to read Laudato Si' even more carefully, without wasting time, and to understand fully its thrust, in the context of mixing religion and environmentalism. (See Chapter V: Syncretism.)

Initial reactions to the Encyclical

When I finally held the 246-paragraph, 183-page, 40,593-word document in hand, and began reading, it seemed that waiting had indeed been the better choice (not mine, but that of the circumstances). In the reading, new issues emerged which I had not thought to address (like world government intervention and socialism as a not-so-hidden agenda.)

Furthermore, a few Catholics, whose insights and opinions I especially value, related that they had no intention of reading the document; a few others did try to read it, but later reported giving up after about 30 pages. I learned that the reasons they abandoned the effort were due to some combination of difficult-to-follow, convoluted language or reasoning, the repetitive nature of certain points, disagreement especially on political issues, including a sensed hostility toward the so-called 'first-world,' an unclear interface between the environment and the agenda for the poor (an undefined term throughout), intimidation by "consensus science," just plain busyness, lack of interest, or other unarticulated reasons.

As I began to read Laudato Si', even greater concerns than 'scientific truth' emerged, i.e. its open advocacy for certain positions which bring us dangerously close to a too-casual alignment with enemies of Catholic Teaching, and the potential for a high level of future risk.

<u>Sustainability concerns</u>

Domestically, the global-warming scenario has been advocated from the highest levels of the U.S. administration which has also pressured for expanded abortion, defended its assault on religious freedom of Catholic organizations which refused to fund contraception and abortion, defended the dismemberment strategies of Planned Parenthood, and insultingly bathed the White House in "rainbow" lights to celebrate the Supreme Court's institutionalizing same-sex unions. In short, any alignment with a government holding positions which advocate what Catholic doctrine identifies as serious sin is dangerous to souls, and a conflict of interest for Catholics.

Surprisingly, the Laudato Si' Encyclical appears to align with individuals and organizations such as the United Nations in its 'sustainability' jargon, a code word for abortion, contraception and euthanasia as strategies to drastically reduce the population of planet Earth. Laudato Si' sadly lacks a clear, firm declaration against those enemies of Catholic Teaching in the many areas in which those advocates and lobbyists are in error. For any of those reasons, and for all of those reasons and more, there was sufficient impetus to analyze the Encyclical and to complete this monograph of concerns.

Infallibility and dialogue

This publication is not offered without my having seriously considered the appropriateness of doing so, and not without substantial prayer and discernment.

Further, it was necessary to examine what permission the Church herself gives to the Faithful to engage in review or criticism of Church documents, especially papal writings, and how those permissions apply in this situation, including in Chapter XII the question of whether or not there are any infallibility claims regarding this Encyclical.

Saintly examples

In Galatians 2:11-21, St. Paul writes of his directly confronting the first pope: ***"But when Cephas came to Antioch I opposed him to his face, because he stood condemned."*** Those were the words of St. Paul when he criticized the first pope (St. Peter) for insincerity in dropping out of table fellowship with the Gentiles when the Jews arrived from Jerusalem. There is a reason these words are included in the Bible and one might suggest that it is to encourage our speaking up for conscience, no matter to whom we are speaking, even a pope.

St. Catherine of Siena likewise spoke out strongly to Pope Gregory XI in his voluntary exile in Avignon, urging him to return to his responsibilities in Rome. In letter 74, for example, she had written: "So take a lesson from the true father and shepherd. For you see that now is the time to give your life for the little sheep who have left the flock. You must seek and win them back by using patience and war—by war I mean by raising the standard of the sweet blazing cross and setting out against the unbelievers. So you must sleep no longer, but wake up and raise that standard courageously."

St. Catherine was unable to read or write, but it did not stop her gentle yet firm style, which finally evoked a papal response for the good of the flock. And one might note its direct, personal message, as opposed to merely theoretical argument.

Canon Law 212 (Ref. E-2)

One particular Canon, especially applicable to expression of opinion to Church leadership by members of the Christian Faithful, is Canon 212, especially Canon 212 §3. The Canon is worth reproducing in its entirety:

- §1. Conscious of their own responsibility, the Christian faithful are bound to follow with Christian obedience those things which the sacred pastors, inasmuch as they represent Christ, declare as teachers of the faith or establish as rulers of the Church.
- §2. The Christian faithful are free to make known to the pastors of the Church their needs, especially spiritual ones, and their desires.
- §3. According to the knowledge, competence, and prestige which they possess, they have the right and even at times the duty to manifest to the sacred pastors their opinion on matters which pertain to the good of the Church and to make their opinion known to the rest of the Christian faithful, without prejudice to the integrity of faith and morals, with reverence toward their pastors, and attentive to common advantage and the dignity of persons.

While it isn't necessary or even possible to apply Canon 212 to every situation, nevertheless there is some comfort in the underlying assumption that laity does indeed have a right ('and even at times the duty') to express opinions on matters for the 'good of the Church.'

<u>**Invitation to dialogue**</u>

Without needing to rely on either saintly precedent or on Canon 212, there is an unusual and explicit invitation in Laudato Si' for dialogue (25x), for debate (12x), and for discussion (6x) on the subjects therein. While one might hesitate to give input, any such reticence is more than compensated by Pope Francis' repeated and mitigating invitation to discuss and debate the matters expressed in Laudato Si'. Since there are few mechanisms within the reach of the laity to engage in such dialogue, and most of us are not likely to be guests of a Synod, our letters, articles, monographs, books and websites are among the relevant current means for achieving such discussion, input and response. I take the Holy Father at his word that he desires such dialogue, and so offer it in this monograph.

The following are examples, with paragraph numbers, of some of Pope Francis' explicit invitations to dialogue and debate:

"We need a conversation which includes everyone ...." (#14)

"...the need for forthright and honest debate ...." (#16)

"...a variety of proposals possible, all capable of entering into dialogue with a view to developing comprehensive solutions." (#60)

"...honest debate must be encouraged among experts, while respecting divergent views." (#61)

"...science and religion, with their distinctive approaches to understanding reality, can enter into an intense dialogue fruitful for both." (#62)

"The Catholic Church is open to dialogue with philosophical thought ...." (#63)

"...this Encyclical welcomes dialogue with everyone so that together we can seek paths of liberation ...." (#64)

If it were not for Pope Francis' invitation to dialogue and debate, I am not sure I would have had the courage to write this review and analysis. If it were not for the Apostle Paul's challenging our beloved first Pope Peter (Cephas) to his face (Galatians Chapter 2), I might have cowered at the thought of disagreeing even on a matter not of 'faith and morals.' And if it were not for the 'moxie' of St. Catherine of Siena, who spoke frankly to Pope Gregory XI, I might have lacked spiritual peace in doing so.

Half a Dialogue

The title **"Half a Dialogue"** recognizes the etymology of the word 'dialogue' from the Greek. The preposition 'dia' means 'through' and 'log' comes from 'logos' or 'word'. Through words we try to convey our thoughts, understanding and concerns. Even if successful, we can each only achieve half of a two-way communication; hence the title **"Half a Dialogue."**

I have tried my best to write in a way respectful of the Holy Father, grateful for his invitation, even though disagreeing with and being disappointed by many things written in Laudato Si'. To the extent that I have failed, I apologize, and will try to correct my words in any subsequent revisions. I give all acknowledgment to the Holy Spirit for leading and sustaining me in anything of value and Truth; all of which is a credit to His patience with me. And I accept all blame for any errors; mistakes are mine alone. An encyclical deserves not only a thorough reading and digestion before commenting, but also prayer for guidance. I have tried to do enough of each.

<u>**Advice on Order of Reading**</u>

Some readers will find it most useful to read straight through **"Half a Dialogue,"** covering first the implications of environmentalism and science regarding faith, then through three major issues and how they relate to Church Teaching (sustainability, subsidiarity and socialism), and then to bringing the teaching 'home' through individual obligations and actions, the need for an enhanced role of the Church, prayers and a summary of concerns addressed to Pope Francis.

Other readers may prefer to skip over the issues of sustainability, subsidiarity and socialism, going right from Chapter VII to Chapter XI, and returning to those three remaining chapters at the end, for deeper understanding. Either approach will work; it is a matter of personal preference.

Chapter I
<u>Introduction and Methodology</u>

Reading Laudato Si' led to a series of on-line posts on <u>www.CleansingFire.org</u>. That blog-site covers a variety of subjects of Catholic interest, especially to traditional, faithful Catholics. Blog posting (for those unfamiliar) benefits from the ability to bring forward an opinion or input much more quickly, to easily make changes and corrections, and to enter into dialogue between writer and reader. Those early posts eventually came to serve as a 'rough draft' for this monograph, **"Half a Dialogue."**

<u>Intellectual cloister</u>

Laudato Si' was signed on May 24, 2015 and released on June 18, 2015. From then until printing of this monograph, other writers' opinions, published widely even by some who had not read the Encyclical in its entirety, were not read, explored, scanned or appropriated in any way. The reason for the separation from the flood of materials, which was generated from various quarters after the release of the Encyclical, was to avoid being influenced by other writers and their analyses, in order to bring a fresh insight and independent approach.

<u>Translation issues</u>

Among the first problems encountered in beginning this project was the need to read the Encyclical as a translation, which places significant weight on the shoulders of the unidentified translators. The reason for assuming more than one translator is that it would be quite negligent to let the Holy Father's words depend upon only one translator, who could easily hijack, with error, personal bias, sloppiness or innuendo, the subtlety and meaning behind the papal writings. There are standard business techniques to eliminate such risk; I hope the Vatican uses those protocols.

Accommodating the organization of the Encyclical

One difficulty, which I encountered throughout the entire study, was the need to re-sort excerpts from somewhat of a horizontal stream-of-consciousness style of the Encyclical into vertical topic areas, developing a matrix to examine the original text on each point. The chapter structure for "**Half a Dialogue**" reorganizes the content by major topic areas, and approximates those matrices or 'vertical slices of content'.

Laudato Si' is not indexed, at least not as of this writing. Therefore, as a service to the readers of "**Half a Dialogue**," Appendix D is a selected word index with paragraph and footnote numbers in the Encyclical, listed for over 100 different words. It was not possible to include every word or phrase of interest. Although a word may not be found on searching the index, a related concept may still occur.

By referring to that word index, the reader will note that the same subject is often widely distributed throughout many different parts of the Encyclical, indicating a different approach in the writing styles. The word index also gives the reader the opportunity to verify excerpted quotes from Laudato Si', and to explore the original context in which they were made. The same Encyclical paragraph may also be referenced more than once, if it touches, for example, on multiple subject areas.

Use of a blog post to develop a topic

The first reading of the Encyclical was completed in its entirety, with margin notes, before publishing anything on-line except the following work plan, which describes in outline form the anticipated subject structure for approaching the task.

Then the rough draft was written on-line, essentially chapter by chapter, as each subtopic was explored, rather than all at once and uploaded piecemeal. Thus, the Laudato Si' series, for as long as it remains on Cleansing Fire, constitutes a virtual on-line first draft of this final monograph. The blog version is approximately 60% of the length of this final monograph word count.

Those subject areas were offered to the blogsite readers to critique. Each installment was published soon after it was finished, section by section, as a 16-part series, over 3 months. All the subjects shown in the original work plan were covered, plus a few others which were raised during the reading of the Encyclical; for example, collectivist concerns, subsidiarity, and certain prayers. The order of presentation of subject areas was changed somewhat to allow for better flow.

Finally, before writing the last chapter, I reread the entire Encyclical, for the sake of verifying tone, meaning, and objectives, and to be sure nothing was overemphasized or underemphasized inappropriately. There were, of course, a number of sections that had to be read multiple times, reflecting the importance of some subjects. Minor changes were made as a result of the additional reading, or due to the need for clarification, and Chapters XIV and XVI were added.

A 10-point prelude for reading Laudato Si' (Ref. E-3)

In advance of reading Laudato Si', realizing that it might be quite controversial, this methodology of approach was published on-line. It reflects the determination not to try to respond point-by-point to the words of the Encyclical, but to form first a framework with which to read and consider the Encyclical in a broader context. Issuing such a prelude also helped me to hold myself accountable publicly for the work plan, and to provide transparency. More important, I considered it a draft to which serious input was welcome.

The following is the original draft framework against which to read and contemplate the Encyclical and to identify the mindset which was brought to the task.

Questions used for initial consideration:

1.   Is there a serious link between the written word and the salvation of souls? If so, how may it be summarized?

2.   Is the Encyclical based on truth? Has any truth, including scientific truth, been compromised for the sake of 'making a point?' Is all opinion clearly differentiable from truth and fact?

3.   Does one sense an abundant love flowing toward the readers, regardless of what position each person holds on the issues, regardless of what each is currently doing or not doing in this matter? Is it unitive rather than divisive?

4.   Is there a suitable mode of humility and shepherdly care to provoke appropriate responses and not to harden hearts?

5.   Is there complete consistency to the governing documents and teachings of the Church, especially the Catechism, Sacred Scripture, Canon Law and similar writings of earlier Popes, not only in quotations but in total context?

6.   Is the order of creation being kept in the right priority, serving the Creator rather than the created?

7.   What are the actionable points at an individual level? What actions or inactions are sins to be confessed, vs. 'nice to do' recommendations that, after due consideration, may be ignored?

8.   Do any teachings of the Encyclical detract either in resources or in priority from any higher duties of each soul? Are there costs in time, energy or resources that would otherwise be compromised by

investing in actions in these matters rather than in higher spiritual priorities?

9.   Does the Encyclical, when fully absorbed, in any way lead toward a 'one-world religion' of environmentalism, of Neo-Pantheism, or encourage substitution of action at an ecclesiastical level, in place of dealing with the urgent moral issues of abortion, euthanasia, anti-biblical gender culture, persecution and annihilation of Christians, especially in the Mid-East?

10.   Is there any danger of syncretism in the words or method of presentation of these writings as an encyclical? Is the content clearly in the 'moral' area covered by infallibility? Or not?

After working in this format for over a month, related subjects evolved: sustainability, subsidiarity, Liberation Theology (Ref. E-4), and collectivism, thus expanding the scope further.

Adapting a blog post to a monograph

One advantage of a blog post is the ability to use color to differentiate various sources of reference material and quotes. It is expensive and hence less practical for paper publishing, but the following conventions will help the reader, especially to identify Encyclical quotes easily.

Text / Commentary — Times New Roman
Reference material — Arial, bold, grey
Sacred Scripture* — Times New Roman, bold italic
Laudato Si' quotes — Lucida Calligraphy

*All scriptural references are to the Revised Standard Version Catholic Edition (RSV-CE) unless otherwise noted.

Capitalization: Pronouns referring to God and to each Person of the Blessed Trinity have been capitalized where possible, including from Sacred Scripture. Such pronouns, in direct quotes from other authors or sources, have not been altered;

5

hence, those pronouns referring to Divine Persons have been left as in the original text.

What does 'n^{th}-world' mean?

The term 'n^{th}-world' is used throughout this monograph. The 'n' is a common term in science, to represent a number, or any number. The 'n' is a common designation given to the word 'number' and yet, in so designating, it is also an unknown quantity, not necessary to specify.

There is a particular awkwardness about contrasting developmental positions of countries often referred to as 'third-world' to what are euphemistically called 'richer' or 'better off' or 'more developed' countries yet, in effect, are seen as 'first-world' countries. But the words slip too facilely. Further, a country may be 'third-world' in its government, but fifth-world in its healthcare, or second-world in its agriculture, but fourth-world in its education. The use of the term 'n^{th}-world' thus applies across a wide range of countries without the need to identify further their infrastructure in any particular area, or to overuse the 'third-world' designation.

The decision to use 'n^{th}-world' as a designator for those who are not 'first-world' is simply to avoid the need to enter into controversy about such status, and to be inclusive of all who do not see themselves as completely 'first-world,' yet allow individual countries the opportunity to position themselves as they choose.

Chapter II
<u>Overview and Impressions</u>

Using the aforementioned framework and orientation, I carefully read the entire Encyclical, Laudato Si', in its British English translation. Obviously, any discussion will be affected by the limitations of the translators, who are not identified, and therefore we are without a track record against which to evaluate the likely accuracy of the translation, not only in content but also in tone. The disastrous track record for the 2014 Synod translation prompts such a disclaimer and concern. There are also certain statements which would benefit from comparison to the Italian and Spanish content of Laudato Si'. There could be benefits from independent retranslation and from reading the footnote references too in their entirety; however, for the sake of this particular commentary, neither has been done, but that fact is called to the reader's attention.

Furthermore, as mentioned in Chapter I regarding maintaining an 'Intellectual Cloister,' the insights of others are not being considered here, of necessity, but should be consulted for a reader's broader view. The deliberate silence of not citing others' comments on the Encyclical neither supports nor opposes those comments.

<u>A suggestion to the reader</u>: if you are intending to read the Encyclical, consider doing so before reading this monograph, so that you too can form your opinion independently.

<u>Footnotes and framework</u>

Many of the footnotes in Laudato Si' are to Pope Francis' own encyclicals or to those of his predecessor popes, or to papal 'catechesis,' or to Bishops' conferences in various parts of the world. Evaluating those original texts might lead to better understanding the context of the present Encyclical, but it is unnecessary to do so in order to explicate Laudato Si'. Pope Francis has made each reference his own by using it in the Encyclical, sometimes attributing his own interpretation, without disputing the content he referenced. There is, however, one exception to this 'rule,' which will be presented in Chapter IX, examining an out-of-context quotation attributed to Pope Benedict XVI.

<u>Lack of footnotes to scientific assertions</u>

In contrast to the footnotes in other papal teachings or in a variety of hierarchical meetings, there is a serious dearth of references and footnotes to scientific claims and to studies or broad allegations regarding the environment; e.g. 'global warming' and 'climate change' are claimed as if they have already been proven. Such statements of 'fact' are not supported by original sources, but rather by prelates' simply making statements on matters not defined as faith or morals.

The percentage of the world claimed to be vulnerable to coastal flooding, and assertions on desertification in Africa, e.g., are not footnoted with the necessary data sources. Unfortunately, such assertion without reference weakens the argument, which is further damaged by appealing to consensus.

Consensus has virtually no value in determining truth. And surrounding scientific claims with references to religious opinions does not boost scientific veracity. There are also no citations or arguments presented to refute critics of 'global warming' and 'climate change,' some of whom are listed in Appendix C. Perhaps it should not be surprising to find almost no technological basis or rationale in an Encyclical which refers to:

"...the assault of the technocratic paradigm." (#111)

Rather, those who would disagree are dealt with as not being sincere or serious; but as *"obstructionist ... nonchalant ... or blind ...."* (#14)

The counterarguments to 'global warming' and 'climate change' assumptions seem to be disregarded in the Encyclical. It is concerning that the fundamental proof sources would be ignored, in a world that is only too ready to dismiss moral truth and turn to what they 'feel' is truth, or 'want' to be truth. Such response can easily masquerade under the guise of the call for

"...a new and universal solidarity ..." (#14), relying on political pressure to launch or enforce or prohibit a program.

Deep disappointment

I am deeply disappointed in Laudato Si', as a Catholic, as an American, and as a person trained in science. My impression is that the Encyclical has a somewhat rambling and haphazard declaration of opinions, at times almost seeming hostile, admixed with a startling collectivist ideology, including challenges to private property rights *(#93)*. However, there is very little that is actionable from a practical point of view. That is not meant as a judgment, but rather raises the question of what is to be the fruit of these efforts. We should always seek the fruit.

Matthew 7:16-20 states: ***"You will know them by their fruits. Are grapes gathered from thorns, or figs from thistles? So, every sound tree bears good fruit, but the bad tree bears evil fruit. A sound tree cannot bear evil fruit, nor can a bad tree bear good fruit. Every tree that does not bear good fruit is cut down and thrown into the fire. Thus you will know them by their fruits."*** From a practical point of view, it is unclear what is hoped to be the fruit of this Encyclical.

An encyclical should have the care of souls in mind

Even after studying the entire Encyclical over several months, and pondering the papal words and intent, I am at a loss to explain, "Why an Encyclical?" Was it simply the vehicle conveniently at hand? The document seems more like a thesis, without data, for a course in environmental activism. It appears to reflect deep-seated concerns and emotional reactions about environmental and ecological issues. Could it have been issued in some other format, such as an Apostolic Exhortation? As a book? It does not create a bridge to communicate with scientists; rather it risks alienating them.

Linking to a claimed but unproven 'global warming' or 'climate change,' Laudato Si' runs the risk of denigrating the seriousness and stature of encyclical communication in the hearts of faithful Catholics, and of 'turning off' those who would otherwise have been open to considering a serious response, by sounding almost like a diatribe. The tone has been a disappointment and one concern is that it may weaken the trust and reliance on future papal promulgations. The Encyclical does not answer the question of where these matters fit in preeminence regarding the needs of souls, and that is an unfortunate omission. So too is the lack of explanation for the seemingly sudden 'urgency,' except if synchronized to world environmental meetings and ecological program schedules.

Is an Encyclical on environment really the highest priority?

Clearly, the care of the physical world is an objective of the Encyclical. The very existence of such an Encyclical implicitly asserts that this is among the most important priorities for a Pope at this time, with his efforts, and with his bully pulpit to the world. And this Encyclical is definitely addressed to the world.

Many Catholics, deeply concerned about the tyranny of secularism, generally do not place these ecological and environmental issues anywhere near the concern level that they do for abortion, euthanasia, same-sex unions, ISIS persecution, abuse of Religious Freedom, human trafficking, the likelihood of martyrdom in current times, and the silence on such matters which 'flat-lines' from the pulpit. There seems to be no effort in the Encyclical to justify the subject matter with regard to such secular urgencies, or to the overarching priority of souls.

Environmental issues do have some importance, but not at the expense of leaving the greatest needs unfilled. In my opinion, if homilies were to begin to preach this Encyclical, in a culture that already short-changes so much which needs to be taught, it would likely impact credibility of the Teaching Office of the Church, and therefore adversely impact souls.

Deeper concern

At times, there is an uncomfortable wording that brings me to a halt over certain sentences, asking "Do I believe that? Is it true?" One Encyclical statement with which I strongly disagree is:

"It is no longer enough, then, simply to state that we should be concerned for future generations. We need to see that what is at stake is our own dignity. Leaving an inhabitable planet to future generations is first and foremost, up to us. The issue is one which dramatically affects us, for it has to do with the ultimate meaning of our earthly sojourn." (#160)

Our dignity? First and foremost? The "ultimate meaning of our earthly sojourn?" I do not believe that the way we leave the physical condition of the planet is the *"ultimate meaning"* of our lives. That specific sentence touches on several areas of concern, to be covered more in the following chapters, especially regarding Pantheism and syncretism. But we read in Revelation that planet earth will not survive the end times, no matter how environmentally pristine, but our souls will, for whichever their destination may be, heaven or hell.

There might have been a way, with a different tone or in a shorter document, to convey the Pope's personal concerns on environmental matters close to his heart, but that clearly did not happen with Laudato Si'. The very length, 40,593 words, including footnotes, all unindexed, makes it difficult for readers to absorb or refer to the content in a meaningful way. A word search (which is approximately correct but may miss an occasional derivative word, or a hyphenated word) indicates the appearance of the word or root "environment" 155x, "techno" 96x, "ecologic" 79x, and the hot button word (un)sustainable 27x. On the other hand, there is reference but once to abortion and 3x to embryo, and not at all to the word euthanasia. There is a surprising lack of Catechism or New Testament references to many of the arguments and opinions set forth in Laudato Si', and missed opportunities, such as not referring to abortion in particular in the following context:

"Every act of cruelty towards any creature is 'contrary to human dignity.'" (#92)

Would this not have been an ideal place to insert language in support of the pro-life activism in the Church?

Difficulty in reading?

There are a number of awkward sentences which are hard to understand, and there also are recently minted eco-terms (like *"rapidification," "deified market"* and *"absolutization"*) that relate to a certain specialization which may fall outside of the understanding of those who don't work in the environmental field. For example, what are we to understand from the sentences:

"A misguided anthropocentrism need not necessarily yield to 'biocentrism,' for that would entail adding yet another imbalance, failing to solve present problems and adding new ones." (#118)

"...humanity has taken up technology and its development according to an undifferentiated and one-dimensional paradigm." (#106)

There are also some words about which scientists might make some reasonable guesses as to their meaning (if not in fields of their own specialization), but which may stump non-scientific laity. Such words may become stumbling blocks to absorbing the meaning of the Encyclical; e.g. *"desertification," "monocultures," "biological corridors," "human ecology," "techno-economic paradigm,"* all without definition. Other references may be outside the experience of some readers, like *"campesino,"* or *"blood diamonds."* We cannot assess if poor translation might have compounded such problems.

The undefined term 'poor'

In the entire New Testament (RSV-CE) the word 'poor' occurs 37x (26x in the Gospels), compared to 61x in this Encyclical. Among the quotes left out of the Encyclical are Christ's own words in Mark 14:7:

"For you always have the poor with you, and whenever you will, you can do good to them; but you will not always have Me." (Briefly also contained in Matthew 26:11 and John 12:8.)

This verse is one of Christ's most straightforward comments on the poor, yet is often ignored in the 'social justice' agenda.

While the word 'poor' seems to be worked into Laudato Si' at every opportunity, sometimes as a non-sequitur, it is not a defined term. Does poor refer to lack of money? power? family?   food?   education?   health?   friends?   job? faith? opportunity? Even Christ used the word in several senses, including *"poor in spirit."* (Matthew 5:3) So, the main thesis, which seems to be that the poor take the brunt of the world's not caring properly for, even abusing, the environment, turns precipitously on the undefined term 'poor' throughout the Encyclical.

Organization of Laudato Si'

The first 5 chapters of Laudato Si' constitute nearly 80% of the Encyclical. Chapter 6 seems to contain a brief summary of the Christian Faith. It has a different tone, and it would be easy to speculate that it had been delegated to a different writer, and that there may be eventual interest in being able to separate the environmental advocacy from subjects of doctrine, such as the Eucharist, Trinity and Our Blessed Mother. Otherwise, why not permeate the exhortations with Church Teaching, rather than compartmentalizing them? We must not be ashamed to bring Christ to the fore, always. *"For whoever is ashamed of Me and of My words, of him will the Son of Man be ashamed when He comes in His glory...."* (Luke 9:26)

It is not useful to rehash further the Laudato Si' chapter format, or to critique line by line, but rather to deal with the macro issues, pointing out, with supporting statements, where the Encyclical veers dangerously close to contradiction or to the peripheries beyond Church teaching. The following chapters will deal with those particular issues, regarding what is most of concern in reading the Encyclical.

Chapter III

<u>Pantheism?</u>

It is the big and underlying question: "Is Environmentalism the road to creating 'One World Religion,' with Pantheism and syncretism the portals through which it will pass? The achievement of 'world peace' has often been equated, at least implicitly, to humans' embracing a single religion, hence valuing the same things and despising the same things, so that no differences exist which divide people or lead to wars.

The impossibility of achieving such a goal of world peace was made clear by Christ:

"And you will hear of wars and rumors of wars; see that you are not alarmed; for this must take place, but the end is not yet." (Matthew 24:6)

But even such a divine statement does not dissuade some proponents from pursuing a fantasy of behavioral (yet intrinsic) change to unite the world in a Utopian Theology, appearing over the ages under different forms, and in more recent times as communism, socialism, aryanism, racism, liberationism, capitalism, and dozens of other 'isms' and now, seemingly at least in some aspects, environmentalism.

Of all the human-created ideologies, over millennia, there is perhaps none so dangerous to individual souls as environmentalism morphed into Pantheism, leading to selected worship of parts of nature. The Old Testament is rife with illustration. And there is no 'Xtreme Environmentalism' so dangerous as that which is foisted by religious leaders as de facto 'religion.' Pantheism (that God is 'in' everything, or God 'is' everything), is easily transformed to worship of anything and everything that is claimed to be the presence of God, i.e.

idolatry, often under the name of 'tolerance.' But, make no mistake, 'One World Religion' means no religion at all, and is a direct danger to souls.

The progressive error: 5 steps in compelling sin

When one takes the first step on a journey, it is well to have the destination in mind. The slippery slope transition from excessive focus on nature to 'One World Religion' looks something like this:

1.   To many people, environmentalism sounds like an appropriate world strategy of tolerance and peace. While some good results might even be achieved in the short term, it institutes a path which deserves attention and concern. The claim that God is (or is 'in') every aspect of the natural world is an emerging Neo-Pantheism which destroys traditional faith.

2.   Pantheism, by which the Chosen People so offended God, repeatedly, in the high groves and even in the temple recesses, is idolatry and violates the First Commandment, making all other commandments easier to transgress.

3.   Syncretism appends aspects of one religion, e.g. 'environmental religion' to true religion, creating a false religion, which is not a religion at all, but is 'validated' by apostates from true religion.

4.   The supposition of 'global warming' and 'climate change' becomes the cover excuse under which we are urged forward onto a spiritually dangerous (but allegedly necessary) path, driving the human community to act, and to act now, without counting the cost, all at the expense of much else that is truly needed for the good of souls.

5.   The sustainability argument, with its avowed intent to reduce population significantly, leads to implementing, forcibly if needed, behavioral and value changes which require imposition of sin -- abortion, euthanasia, same-sex unions, embryonic experimentation, and gender distortion in order to achieve its objectives.   Then the society in transition moves from 'allowing' individual preferences to requiring all members to abet and fund what is sinful.   And the path can be very rapid.

After all, it is a downhill slide on the slippery slope; very few people 'slide up' the slope. If 'compelling sin' sounds absurd, consider bakers who refuse to bake a cake being fined over $100,000, or a public employee jailed for refusing to sign a 'marriage license' which violates her faith. Or consider doctors not licensed unless they have performed abortions, thus being restricted from a medical career. Consider even the elderly, obligated to carry insurance for abortion, contraception, gender reassignment, and – soon – euthanasia (to provide for their own demise first with their lifetime savings and family inheritances, then with their bodies). The unthinkable of forced abortion to enforce one-child families has already been in place in China for years. It is not about the threat of the future; it is about the reality of the present, in various countries. (See information links in Appendix F.) It is about the ripening of the world to receive the harvesting sickle. (Revelation 14:15)

The physical world was created to serve humans, not humans to serve the environment

The history of mankind, as recorded in Sacred Scripture and in the fragments of the earth's own archeological record, provides relevant exegesis. In Genesis 1:26, God proclaims:

"Let Us make man in Our image, after Our likeness; and let them have dominion over the fish of the sea, and over the

presence 'must not be contrived but found, uncovered.'"
(#225)

Humans are stewards of creation, neither objects to be controlled, nor the ultimate controllers

Human power is not absolute; God gives conditions and He, Himself, deigns to intervene as He chooses -- either with the cooperation of humans, as in preserving creation aboard Noah's Ark, or without human cooperation as in the creation of the universe, so clearly articulated to Job in Chapter 38:31: ***"Can you bind the chains of the Pleiades?"*** The oldest book of the Bible, Job, brings forth the message not only of God's singular role in Creation, but that more is expected from people of faith. Reading Chapters 37-39 of Job ought to convince us that God is in charge of the weather too, that there is no point at which He handed it over to humans, even if He lets us try to play with it from time to time. God reminds us of man's lack of power. To aspire to usurp God's power can itself be a form of idolatry – idolatry of self.

"But the mountain falls and crumbles away, and the rock is removed from its place; the waters wear away the stones; the torrents wash away the soil of the earth; so Thou destroyest the hope of man." (Job 14:18-19)

Of course, God's ultimate intervention at His own initiative is the Son of God's entrance into human history, from Manger to Cross to Resurrection. God has not abandoned His work; we *are* His work. All creation is His work. The environment serves the work of God. And the Hand of God frequently uses, or at least permits, His Presence and Power to be manifested through the environment, especially through weather and climate, powers which hitherto He has not shared with humans (nor seems by any scriptural reference to be planning to do so.) Weather and climate, in particular, are ways in which God reminds us that He is God. We are not. We are cautioned to deal with it. It is understandable, perhaps, that the illusion of being able to control climate should possess people at a time when they are turning away from God toward themselves.

The prerogatives of God

The metaphorical analogy is instantly recognizable as the human obligation to prepare and to endure rather than to covet control of that which is out of the hands of the created. The Bible, both Old and New Testaments, is replete with such demonstrations of God's power through wind and rain, earthquakes, droughts and floods. Nowhere is that power given into the hands of the human race, except under God's strict scrutiny and direction, (as when Elijah was permitted to shut up the skies, for years, to stop the rain, in 1 Kings 17).

Nature is used by God for His own purposes, whether it involves thousands of years of animal sacrifice, or a demonstration of His power in the dry-shod crossing of the Red Sea or, in the New Testament, when Christ permits about 2000 demon-infested swine to go over a cliff to their drowning, to illustrate the reality of demon possession (Mark 5:1-20). Even in ancient Egypt Joseph's prophecy of seven fat years and seven lean years called for stewardship in the management of storehouses for the protection of human life. Weather has cycles, within and beyond human lifetimes and beyond natural human abilities, demanding our faith and trust. Christ Himself, in calming the storm and the waters (Mark 4:36-41), made that event a matter of Faith, not a matter of human control and, by implication, the need for Faith in all the storms of life, "weather or not."

One interpretation of John 3:7-9 is that Nicodemus is taken to task for *not* acknowledging that God is the One Who makes the weather happen, and if we don't understand the basics about weather, how will we understand anything else as being under God's power?

"The wind blows where it wills, and you hear the sound of it, but you do not know whence it comes or whither it goes; so it is with every one who is born of the Spirit. Nicodemus said to Him, 'How can this be?' Jesus answered him, 'Are you a teacher of Israel, and yet you do not understand this?'"

For a teacher of souls not to understand even the source of power over the weather, as simple as the wind, is shocking! Yes, indeed. God does not bid us to try to control the weather, but rather to trust in Him. We need to beware of the age-old error of man's self-esteem seeking to be like unto God, including his desire to control even the weather.

Let us be clear. This is not to say that humans aren't capable of abusing the environment, or acting irresponsibly. The point is not any criticism of good stewardship of the earth, cleaning it up or minimizing future pollution. Rather, the concern is about acting as if, by our own actions (or the lack of our actions), we can change the weather and climate, heretofore all God's prerogative. Full understanding regarding natural disaster is beyond human ability; weather and climate belong to God's direct power and to His Will. The question is if we are going to need to learn that lesson one more time.

Furthermore, none of these observations in any way eliminates the ordinary need to value life, to build natural protections like sea walls, dams and dikes, to irrigate the land and rotate crops or derive drinking water from the sea. We have permission to use what we have been given. We are called to build strong foundations to withstand the storm in body and spirit.

God tells us, e.g. in Luke 6:48, that to act upon His words is to be *"...like a man building a house, who dug deep, and laid the foundation upon rock; and when a flood arose, the stream broke against that house, and could not shake it, because it had been well built."*

And none of these observations relieves us of the need or obligation to pray always to stay in the Hands of a Loving God.

Is Neo-Pantheism at the root of climate control efforts?

Neo-Pantheism today may appear more sophisticated than the Pantheism of old, through machinations of cyber-analysis, space station monitoring, multi-variate calculus; i.e. the god of technology. Such Neo-Pantheism is still evolving, and will be more identifiable in hindsight. Pantheism includes either 1) the aspect that God is the rock, the river, the cloud, and is therefore given worship out of fear, ignoring His transcendent power and majesty beyond what is of immediate need to the worshiper, or 2) that if God is so 'accessible' in nature, then He can be 'managed' or manipulated by controlling nature and our resources; i.e. that God really isn't God at all. The first is reminiscent of the argument that "I don't need to go to Church on Sunday morning; I experience God on the golf course or fishing." It is closer to the 'old Pantheism.' The other argument is that "I don't need God; I'm in charge of my life and I can handle it. I can even handle His job of managing the weather, either destroying it by my extreme pollution, or saving it through governmental edict." That approach is closer to environmentalism's just trumping all worship of God, substituting the created person or object in place of God.

Neo-Pantheism may not sound like the errors of old; but there are many similarities. Today, the edge of Neo-Pantheism is more canted toward trying to manipulate God, sometimes by ignoring Him, forgetting there are still rights and powers reserved to God, and that there are still consequences for trespass.

<u>Revisiting the Tower of Babel</u>

In the current governmental efforts to control weather and effect 'climate control,' there is a certain similarity to the megalomaniac building of the Tower of Babel and its associated punishments. Did the onlookers, who cheered the tower builders and touted their claims, suffer the same fate of division, separation and discord? We can wonder. It is, at least in part, our awesome inability to control weather that reminds us of the higher Power. And, perhaps, when God does punish in kind, we might consider the possibility, as onlookers, that weather-related disasters may worsen, as both punishment and benevolent warning. What exactly is mankind trying to do in 'controlling' the weather but usurping God-powers?

But we can be ignorant as a people, even when God seems to be clearly working; like Nicodemus we can't read the signs. For example, in autumn 2012, New York State was avidly planning and pushing forward an agenda of abortion up to the moment of birth; pro-lifers were praying it wouldn't pass but it seemed *impossible* to prevent.

On October 28, Hurricane Sandy struck at the heart of New York City, in a spot never before so devastated by a hurricane, resulting in 53 deaths and $32 billion in property damage. Most people see no connection to the legislative agenda which was being formulated at that time. The storm struck on the Feast of St. Jude, Patron Saint of Impossible Causes. That bill did not pass. Connected or not? Who can say? Perhaps our contact with the earth and the weather is so alienated that we no longer even ask the question of whether or not God has intervened.

"For when Thy judgments are in the earth, the inhabitants of the world learn righteousness." (Isaiah 26:9b)

Is the sustainability initiative inevitable?

In Chapter VIII, we consider that Pantheism is strongly and particularly aligned with the modern sustainability concepts, elevating the environment over human life, for the sake of those more 'worthy' of life, in the eyes, of course, of those who deem themselves 'worthiest.' This is particularly appealing to those who live rejecting the virtue of humility, who see problems as a shortage of self-esteem, and who principally seek the very immortalization of themselves, by themselves, an ultimate grinning 'selfie' surfing on a tide of millions dead.

The gross concepts of sustainability are rife throughout the Encyclical. If one believes, as some supporters of sustainability are reported to do, that the planet can only sustain one or two billion people and we have 7 billion currently on earth, there is an implicit assertion that the environment is more important than the souls God created, except for those selected as being 'worthy' not to be culled. There is some very dangerous territory of sustainability attaching itself to Laudato Si', without much questioning of the assertions, and that also leaves open a door through which pantheistic principles can enter.

Conflict in utilization of resources

A redirection of the efforts of humankind to major environmental enhancement, especially to those weather-related, necessarily takes energy, resources and effort away from that which is needed more: preaching the Gospel, care of souls, saving babies from abortion, protecting the elderly from euthanasia. Such redirection inevitably focuses on coveting the power to change climate, rather than on the gifts or grace of God's favor, and can become a tyranny that expects dedication to Mother Earth rather than to Father God, with the concomitant inability to serve two masters.

<u>**Reflection**</u>

On first reading of the Encyclical, I experienced a brief uplifting mindset in the poetic prayer of St. Francis of Assisi, as he addressed all of creation in familial terms, like

"Sister, Mother Earth." (#1)

Later, those terms used without an aura of poetry seem more focused on earth than heaven. In rereading, there is less of a sense of uplifting, and more of a sense of a certain 'heaviness' and oppressive tone, recounting myriad problems weighing on Mother Earth, with very little optimism.

I was finally able to identify the disconnect I experienced in the words and expectations of Pope Francis, who has been seen on the world stage with smiles, and a certain personally joyful image. However, Laudato Si' seems ponderous and repetitive and, at times, even angry, with a distinct lack of joy, a bold contrast to the words of St. Francis, a very different persona. There is a sense of being in the control of a harsh world rather than a loving Father Who has a real interest in us and in the world He created but Who refuses to be controlled.

Such an emotional draining made it difficult to persist in reading Laudato Si'. It can also be frustrating that there is so little that individuals are called to do, as individuals. More than ever, we seem to need a sense of hope; but hope does not lie in man-made strategies, or in carrying out government initiatives, but rather in seeking to be always in the Will of God.

Chapter IV
<u>One World Religion</u>

It is absolutely necessary to open this section with a statement that I neither believe Pope Francis is a Pantheist, nor that he has a hidden agenda to cooperate with global forces which are undermining true religion and pushing toward 'One World Religion.' However, I am of the opinion that such global forces are willingly taking advantage of the Teaching Office of the Church, and using Pope Francis' sincerity, influence and prestige on their own chessboard. And, in that realm of earthly powers, sadly it appears that the Pope could become more of a pawn than a king.

The direct quotes from Laudato Si' in this chapter excerpt the threat and the momentum which are building for pantheistic 'religion,' already using the Encyclical as argument and testimony. These quick glimpses, at least of the language, if not also the practice, seem to reflect a neo-pantheistic view. Its stretching of meaning could be viewed as poetry, but only in a limited sense, and not, it seems, in a document mostly lacking in the poetic. It is difficult in reading Laudato Si' to balance the darker, more pessimistic words with the occasional bursts of the poetic, but it is only fair to report both. Which part is more Pope Francis is a complicated discernment, which contributes to the impression of multiple authors. Waiting for a glimpse of Pope Francis' own views, his peering at us through the paragraphs, is a bit like catching the next quick appearance of the director in Alfred Hitchcock movies. There is a flash, and then he is gone again.

The following language is not offered as being comprehensive, but just as examples that need far more explanation than is given in the Encyclical. If a text is only poetic, the reader reaches one conclusion. If it is changing or re-interpreting doctrine, then a different conclusion is reached. A transition in tone builds as the Encyclical moves from lower paragraph numbers to higher, from the more obvious and accepted, to what is more novel to our common understanding:

"The entire material universe speaks of God's love, his boundless affection for us. Soil, water, mountains: everything is ... a caress of God." (#84)

"To sense each creature singing the hymn of its existence is to live joyfully in God's love and hope .... This contemplation of creation allows us to discover in each thing a teaching which God wishes to hand on to us, since 'for the believer, to contemplate creation is to hear a message, to listen to a paradoxical and silent voice.'" (#85)

"Everything is related, and we human beings are united as brothers and sisters on a wonderful pilgrimage, woven together by the love God has for each of his creatures and also which unites us in fond affection with brother sun, sister moon, brother river and mother earth." (#92)

"Inner peace is closely related to care for ecology ...." *(#225)* This is a challenging observation. Isn't inner peace about being in a state of grace?

"In order to make society more human, more worthy of the human person, love in social life - political, economic and cultural - must be given renewed value, becoming the constant and highest norm for all activity." (#231)

"When we feel that God is calling us to intervene with others in these social dynamics, we should realize that this too is part of our spirituality, which is an exercise of charity and, as such, matures and sanctifies us." (#231) Such words might seem simply poetical were they not

transitioning to the syncretistic words of Chapter V. We may not see this, because we don't expect such word combinations to be in papal writings.

Our own naïveté can be a stumbling block for us. Luke 16:8 states: *"...the sons of this world are more shrewd in dealing with their own generation than the sons of light."* Knowing this, Christ cautions in Matthew 10:16: *"Behold, I send you out as sheep in the midst of wolves; so be wise as serpents and innocent as doves."* The question is not so much if the wolves are targeting the sheepfold, but to what extent they are already breaking into it. (This is not inconsistent with Pope Paul VI's famous comment on the Smoke of Satan entering the Church.)

Serious as is any attempt to wrest God's own powers from Him, such as by pursuing the ability to control climate and weather, there is an even more catastrophic misuse of the environment, and that is in worshiping it, i.e. idolatry. Since Pantheism sees the environment as being God, it inevitably speeds forward to acts of worship. Well-documented in biblical history, pantheistic worship is a severe affront to God, who revealed Himself as Creator and later, in fullness, as Father. Thus, it is worth revisiting the sad past of humankind, and its willingness to sink into Pantheism.

Inherent Pantheism?

Historic Pantheism is not without rationale. In some sense, it is almost an inherent response to nature in a spiritual void. If people do not know the True and Saving God, they understandably turn for control of natural forces to various types of Pantheism, to the beauty of the earth, to so-called gods of agriculture, water, and harvest to bring blessings and abate disaster. The Aztecs, for example, pursued human sacrifice to their own cosmological gods to appease a supposed thirst for blood. Pantheism thus becomes the major source of a multiplicity of gods, and it is difficult (but unnecessary here) to make explicit distinction among the forms.

God clearly speaks His judgment upon those who knowingly replace His rightful role with idol worship. In Leviticus 26:29-30, the Lord tells Moses that the punishment will include cannibalization of their offspring, pestilence and sword, and seven times punishments for the sin: *"You shall eat the flesh of your sons, and … your daughters. And I will destroy your high places, and cut down your incense altars, and cast your dead bodies upon the dead bodies of your idols; and my soul will abhor you."* In Ezekiel 6:6, God promises: *"Wherever you dwell your cities shall be waste and your high places ruined, so that your altars will be waste and ruined, your idols broken and destroyed, your incense altars cut down, and your works wiped out."*

<u>Reaping the Whirlwind?</u>

Let us ask, at least this once, if the sordid environment, which Laudato Si' claims is now inflicted on the world, is not reminiscent of and justified by the curse that *"Your cities shall be waste,"* and if it is not ludicrous to try to repair the damage of God's curse before we repair our hearts?

Can we seriously justify hundreds of millions of dead, aborted babies as not deserving a memorial that the cities of the earth should be laid to waste? Can an environmental revitalization be the answer to wallowing in the waste? Just clean up our mess and move on? Really? Is this not, in itself, a move to justify a religion of nature, which requires no admission of wrong doing, no uncomfortable and judgmental God, no doctrinal expectations? Must we make the point that the modern-day idol is the self-esteem lifestyle to which prospective mothers yield themselves up on the abortion table?

The Role of the Clergy

We need look no further than the Golden Calf incident at Mt. Sinai to realize how quickly human hearts turn to worshiping animal idols, including their own animal instincts. Further, we note how influential their religious leader, Aaron, was in the process of their demise! (Exodus, Chapter 32)

It is understandable that such affront to God cannot occur without the support, encouragement, connivance and ignorance of the priestly class. Even great leaders are drawn into what the priestly class does not adequately condemn. Solomon's downfall was not that he had so many wives, but that he catered to their pagan gods. In 1 Kings 3:3 we read: ***"Solomon loved the Lord, walking in the statutes of David his father; only, he sacrificed and burnt incense at the high places."*** Solomon's love for the Lord did not keep him from idolatry.

After the split of the Northern Kingdom from the tribes in the south, the Northern Kings engineered worship sites to keep their people from making pilgrimage to the Temple in Jerusalem. Indeed, it was not only the priestly class who misled the people, but also the civil leaders who forcibly implemented idolatry for their own purposes. Politics interfering with religious worship is not a new concept.

Once established, the high places were virtually impossible to eradicate, even for a determined, righteous king, although a few later tried. Idol worship became a repeated future source of contaminating the Chosen People, whether those idolatrous temptations were sources of sexual revelry, or the desolate consummation in fiery sacrifice of their own children. Thus we have centuries of proof how, once established, pantheistic worship, which is easily formed, is very difficult to eliminate. And it is the same reason why we should now, assiduously, guard against its intrusion, from any source, and especially through the Church. Clergy, however, have greater power than politicians, because they can mislead through their silence. Therefore, the obligation to speak Truth from the pulpit weighs heavily on the shoulders of the ordained. It is not a question of being divisive or not; it is a question of being faithful.

Pantheism in Antiquity

The idolatrous activities among the Chosen People in the Northern Kingdom were, in effect, encouraged by hundreds of false priests, pagan priests, who curried favor with King Ahab and Jezebel. The lies of pseudo-religious leaders provoked true prophets like Elijah to resist, challenge and condemn, and to be God's instrument to drive them out. The idolatrous people and the false prophets and priests seem to have mutually tolerated each other, as long as neither called the other to repentance. But a true prophet, acting in accordance with God's Will, can only give a holy message which cannot be ignored. It can be rejected, but not imagined as unheard.

Environmentalism today exhibits some of the same features which made it hard to eradicate the high places and idols. The locales were likely beautiful spots, surrounded by the awesome wonder of what God Himself had created. The contrast between beautiful and ugly externals can turn hearts and become a motive unto itself. Man's inability to duplicate the majesty of nature by his own power may be part of the fascination, seeking God but not fully yielding to Him.

Yet, people involved in idol worship in antiquity must have felt that they had at least some power in their hands, that they could create outcomes by their own efforts, their own sacrifices, dances, cutting of flesh, ritualistic orgies offered to a higher power. Some of the 'means' may be different today, but community participation is still demanded and the lie, that we control God through our own efforts, persists.

Christians died for their refusal to sacrifice to the denizens of the Roman Pantheon. It was not so much because of the Romans' rejection of Christ, but because His followers would countenance no other God, and refused to sacrifice to a wide range of 'gods' worshiped by Romans. In Greece, St. Paul found the Agora (marketplace) in Athens filled with 'gods,' one of which was named the 'unknown god.' St. Paul appropriated it for his own teaching purposes (Acts 17:23) to introduce Christ. Thus, well after the time of Christ, and as Christianity spread, idolatry festered too, for the challenge is not so much to rid it from a country or a territory, but rather to rid it from the human heart. It is the same challenge today.

Post-modern Pantheism

One can hardly blame those who are ignorant of the true God for their misguided attempts to mitigate disaster. Even today, otherwise intelligent people (who have scant credibility to assert they are ignorant of the true God except through their own willfulness), set up sports and movie stars as their 'gods,' and money and power and sexual pleasure as well. They fear rousing the ire of their mini 'god' called 'luck,' and seek some measure of control, like charting horoscopes, wearing 'lucky clothing,' using enneagrams, reading tarot or 'knocking on wood.' The level of such offense may seem minor, until one considers against Whom the offense is committed and how deeply inbred and persistent is the error.

Should we not expect that the modern human would have progressed beyond the obsession to worship the environment, especially after 2000 years of Christianity? In a primitive people to whom God has not been revealed, worship of the environment might be understood, but to those who are highly educated? Technological leaders? Having every modern advantage and benefit of exploring the deepest thoughts and writings of the ages? In some ways, it defies imagination! In other ways, it simply reminds us of how human pride seeks control, and is vulnerable to that which lures it with the lie of power or at least the promise to overlook its sin.

We must remember too that this call to manage weather and climate has not originated among superstitious n^{th}-world people, but among those who want to be seen as the intellectual elite. Greek tragedy is still relevant: **"Whom the gods would destroy, they first make mad."** (Attributed to various individuals, including Euripides.)

Environmentalism -- path to pantheistic and syncretistic 'One World Religion'?

The sweep toward a worldwide religion ultimately seeks to gather everyone into uniformity of worship, dropping that which is a source of dissent, rebelling against the previously respected religious authorities and tenets, and attracting to the core those most favoring permissiveness toward sin, especially sexual sin. But the permissiveness is inevitably toward all but those who disagree and hold to God's higher values, with righteousness now called 'intolerance' or 'hate' by those pushing forward to a one-world pseudo-religion, i.e. a state religion.

Ironic as it may seem, what is most needed to successfully impel a secular crusade toward an environment-based religion is endorsement by leading religious leaders and none would be more of a 'coup' than the Pope. His power would be the most significant of all, manifested by high-level commitment, such as in an Encyclical, and by ignoring moral issues competing for worldwide attention, cooperation or repentance, issues which are much less 'popular,' but far more convicting.

At first it might seem counter-intuitive to claim that a false religion needs 'religious leaders,' but 'converting' those who are presently leaders then co-opts them into the movement, removes them as a true resource to the people of God, blocks their escape, and enables the disguise of what is not worship of God to be accepted as a kind of modern worship, validated by those already accepted as religious leaders.

The Holy Spirit does protect God's Church, but not necessarily particular members of the hierarchy, personally. Otherwise it would be difficult to explain 'bad popes,' or prelates covering up child-abuse offenses.

The culture of death already holds sway, with abortion and euthanasia as its post-modern offerings. Thus, the endorsement by religious figures of 'One World Religion' is mandatory for its spread, as the portal to such mindset unification, closing the gates of escape to those religious leaders and their flocks, fastening their chains, and paving the way for persecution of those who don't 'convert.'

The Really Good News

We know that the gates of hell will not prevail against the Church founded by Christ even if every heretical or spin-off denomination should cave in, even if every leader should fail.

"And I say also unto thee, that thou art Peter, and upon this rock I will build My church; and the gates of hell shall not prevail against it." (KJV, Matthew 16:18).

Christ never promised it would be easy. In Luke 18:8 Christ asks: *"...when the Son of Man comes, will He find faith on earth?"* Perhaps, in more recent times, we even understand why He asked the question.

Chapter V

<u>Syncretism?</u>

"Religious syncretism, the fusion of diverse religious beliefs and practices."   Encyclopedia Britannica

Syncretism is, at heart, an unequal yoking. The authentic Catholic Church proceeds very carefully to avoid syncretism, which can lead to a dilution or misrepresentation of our Faith. For example, in Haiti there has been a long-standing problem of some syncretists' trying to inculcate voodoo practices into the Mass and other liturgies, and that is not allowed. However, in Africa, where dancing at Church services is historic practice, accommodations are made to allow for that joyful expression to continue on the part of attendees, such as in their bringing forth their offerings, but not to become Liturgy itself. When North American culture tries to graft on legitimate parts of another culture, and to transform bona fide African joyful processional dancing into liturgical dance in the aisles of a city Cathedral, even if it didn't violate local norms, it would still look just plain silly!

Syncretism is far more serious than just looking silly. Even for one without any deep theological training, it is not difficult to point out what is disturbing in Laudato Si'; i.e., what evokes an aura of juxtaposing holy language and serving the worship of God, to what is common, secular, and materialistic, serving the environment or the social agenda on its own terms. The meaning of words, which we have come to know belong to our Catholic Faith, are destabilized when used almost as 'selling points' to push a separate agenda.

Although it is impossible to read the intentions behind Laudato Si's word choices, which convey, or at least stir, thoughts of syncretism, nevertheless it is possible and necessary to identify the text which causes the discomfort, and to caution that such statements not be blithely accepted as elevating the created to an inappropriate dignity.

Although some phrases are carefully attributed to other writers, even to Pope Saint John Paul II, their repeated use in Laudato Si' makes them also Pope Francis' own words of authorship. The 'context' of references has not been verified (except for one example regarding subsidiarity in Chapter IX.)

It is not unrealistic to sense some 'hijacking' of the sacred, for purposes which are secular. Shown below are seemingly syncretistic examples from Laudato Si'; the problematic language is **bolded** for quick identification, and frames these issues using religious terms in a way different from the Catechism, Sacred Scripture and Canon Law. Confusion in Faith causes risk to souls. The following is a selection of excerpts from Laudato Si' to illustrate the disturbing juxtaposition:

*"...global ecological **conversion.**"(#5)*

*"...the need for each of us to **repent** of the ways we have harmed the planet ..." (#8)*

*"...acknowledge our **sins against creation** ..." (#8)* The idea of 'sinning against creation' or 'sinning against the environment' are rather questionable concepts. In Psalm 51 David calls out to God for mercy and cleansing of his sins. He says the fascinating words in verse 4: **"Against Thee, Thee only, have I sinned...."** With "Thee only," and in spite of the horrendous wrongs against Bathsheba and her husband Uriah the Hittite, which David committed, the Psalm is not applying the Hebrew word *chata'* except to a sin against God. It is very instructional for us, because when we lose the sense of sin, as being against God Himself, we begin diluting the impression of that sin with other wrongs, even crimes against other humans,

and lose perspective on the immense seriousness of sin against God. And using language like "sins against the environment' elevates the created world to a dignity it does not deserve. The point is that the language of the Psalm differentiates; when we do commit a wrong against another person, the wrong is against that person; the sin is against God. (Of course, it still needs confession and repentance for the sin, and appropriate restitution to the person wronged.)

"...to commit a crime against the natural world is a sin against ourselves ..." (#8) See foregoing comment.

"As Christians, we are also called 'to accept the world as a sacrament of communion ....'" (#9)

"...We learn to see ourselves in relation to all other creatures: 'I express myself in expressing the world; in my effort to decipher the sacredness of the world, I explore my own.'" (#85)

"A sense of deep communion with the rest of nature cannot be real if our hearts lack tenderness, compassion and concern ...." (#91)

"We human beings are united as brothers and sisters on a wonderful pilgrimage ...." (#92)

"Covenant between Humanity and the Environment" (#209)

"Ecological Conversion" (#216 to #221)

"The ecological conversion needed to bring about lasting change is also a community conversion." (#219)

"...splendid universal communion ..." (#220)

*"...an ecological **conversion** can inspire us to greater creativity and enthusiasm in resolving the world's problems and in offering ourselves to God 'as a living sacrifice, holy and acceptable.'"* (#220) Reference is to Romans 12:1, but it seems fair here to note that Romans continues with **"...which is your spiritual worship. Do not be conformed to this world but be transformed by the renewal of your mind, that you may prove what is the will of God, what is good and acceptable and perfect."** The use in Laudato Si' does not seem to support the spiritual worship intent or the context of these verses in the Letter to the Romans. Personally, I am very uncomfortable juxtaposing words from Sacred Scripture and its implicit allusion to the Mass to the idea of an "Ecological Conversion."

*"We ... understand our superiority ... as a different capacity which, in its turn, entails a serious responsibility stemming from our **faith**."* (#220) – This seems to be a very tenuous leap at best, since our difference from other creatures is intrinsic; not as a different capacity; i.e. we are made in the image and likeness of God.

*"...**sublime** fraternity with all creation."* (#221)

*"Care for nature is part of a lifestyle which includes the capacity for living together and **communion**."* (#228)

*"When we feel that God is calling us to intervene with others in these social dynamics, we should realize that this too is **part of our spirituality**, which is an exercise of **charity** and, as such, matures and **sanctifies** us."* (#231)

*"...community actions, when they express self-giving love, can also become **intense spiritual experiences**."* (#232)

"Sacramental Signs and the Celebration of Rest" (#233)

Quoting a Muslim Sufi mystic?

Laudato Si' then introduces text from the Muslim writer Ali al-Khawas, with a number of direct quotes. Wikipedia (always subject to revision) states the following:

"In 2015 he [al-Khawas] was cited by the Roman Catholic Pope Francis in his encyclical Laudato si' on the topic of ecology. Francis writes that humanity can 'discover God in all things.'"

"The ideal is not only to pass from the exterior to the interior to discover the action of God in the soul, but also to discover God in all things." (#233)

Laudato Si' credits al-Khawas for the concept of nature's *"'mystical meaning,' to be found in a leaf, in a mountain trail, in a dewdrop, in a poor person's face." (#233) [159]*

Laudato Si' states: *"The spiritual writer Ali al-Khawas stresses from his own experience the need not to put too much distance between the creatures of the world and the interior experience of God. As he puts it: 'Prejudice should not have us criticize those who seek ecstasy in music or poetry. There is a subtle mystery in each of the movements and sounds of this world. The initiate will capture what is being said when the wind blows, the trees sway, water flows, flies buzz, doors creak, birds sing, or in the sound of strings or flutes, the sighs of the sick, the groans of the afflicted ...'" [159]*

Why was a 9th century Muslim Sufi poet and mystic chosen for the key message in this section?   [St. Bonaventure and St. John of the Cross are next quoted, but briefly]. Is bringing Sufism into proximity to the two saints, secondarily mentioned, also a risk of syncretism? While contemplative prayer is open to those who have received such a gift from God, we should remember that those great saints were well grounded in Catholicism before, during and after their experiences. There would seem to be little basis to analogize or combine their experiences with cultures which do not accept Christ, just for the sake of an environmental encyclical.

Remaining quotes, potentially syncretistic, are disturbing

"The Sacraments are a privileged way in which nature is taken up by God to become a means of mediating supernatural life. Through our worship of God, we are invited to embrace the world on a different plane." (#235)

Speaking of the Eucharist, Laudato Si' says of Christ: *"He comes not from above but from within .... The Eucharist ... embraces and penetrates all creation ...." (#236)* It is difficult to understand how this is said. Christ <u>did</u> come from above. John 3:31 states: ***"He who comes from above is above all; he who is of the earth belongs to the earth and of the earth he speaks: He who comes from heaven is above all. He bears witness to what He has seen and heard, yet no one receives His testimony, he who receives His testimony sets his seal to this, that God is true."*** One might even see Laudato Si' as being 'of the earth.' So how can Laudato Si' say that Christ did not come from above?

"The Eucharist is also a source of light and motivation for our concerns for the environment, directing us to be stewards of all creation." (#236) The Church has carefully honed and passed on to us the specific and accurate language surrounding the Eucharist. While we should continue to speak of that miracle in praise and thanksgiving, great care should be taken not to introduce "alternative" ways of speaking which can easily cause confusion, and thus denigration. Clarity, not confusion, belongs to the Holy Spirit.

"And so the day of rest, centred on the Eucharist, sheds it [sic] light on the whole week, and motivates us to greater concern for nature and the poor." (#237)

"...the challenge of trying to read reality in a Trinitarian key." (#239)

"The human person grows more, matures more and is sanctified more to the extent that he or she enters into relationships to live in communion with God, with others and with all creatures. In this way, they make their own that trinitarian dynamism which God imprinted in them when they were created. Everything is interconnected, and this invites us to develop a spirituality of that global solidarity which flows from the mystery of the Trinity." (#240)

"... crucified poor ..." (#241)

Conclusion

There is very little additional commentary to be made regarding the risk of syncretism. The quotes stand for themselves, so most of them have been included. One cannot speculate on the motive in using, in such a way, so many words which have a particular meaning in Catholicism. We can only note the effect, which I personally find very disturbing. It seems to leave too much room open for incoherent or dissident interpretations, troubling the unity mark of the Church, and opening yet another door to 'One World Religion.'

If we were just dealing with one or two instances of 'misspeaking,' a juxtaposition of Catholic words to the environmental vocabulary, it could be argued 'bad translation,' or an oversight. But the sheer volume of instances, spread through so many sections of Laudato Si', points to a different scenario, one to which attention must be drawn.

One must be especially careful in using these references with the 'little ones' — souls of any age who would be troubled and confused in their faith by such references, lest these phrases become stumbling blocks. Even St. Paul said in Romans 14:13: ***"Then let us no more pass judgment on one another, but rather decide never to put a stumbling block or hindrance in the way of a brother."*** For example, even to hear from the pulpit such syncretistic words might lead to misunderstanding, harm, or scandal.

If syncretism were to be used, under the guise of religious leadership, in a transition from environmentalism to pantheistic worship, it might look somewhat similar to such juxtaposition of holy words to those of more common usage.

And, so, let us remember St. Paul's words (Galatians 4: 8-9): ***"Formerly, when you did not know God, you were in bondage to beings that by nature are no gods: but now that you have come to know God, or rather to be known by God, how can you turn back again to the weak and beggarly elemental spirits, whose slaves you want to be once more?"***

Chapter VI
<u>Truth Matters in Theology and Science</u>

Jesus Christ is *"...the Way, and the Truth and the Life"* (John 14:6). The word 'truth' is used 21 times in the Gospel of John.

<u>Who or what is Truth?</u>

Lack of Truth leads to bad judgment, and leaves little room to reverse judgment. We need look no further than Christ's standing before Pilate to see the abuse and error which open up when one ignores the abyss of lies and innuendo, especially to please an audience. The expectations of the audience become part of the pressure not to recant.

In an infamous passage in the Gospel of John 18:37-38 Pilate speaks to Christ: *"...'So you are a king?' Jesus answered, 'You say that I am a king. For this I was born, and for this I have come into the world, to bear witness to the truth. Every one who is of the truth hears My voice.' Pilate said to Him, 'What is truth?' After he had said this, he went out to the Jews again, and told them, 'I find no crime in Him.'"* Then, as we know, Pilate sent Jesus to the Cross. It is one thing to know the Truth; it is another to live our lives as witnesses to Truth (which cannot be compromised without alienating our relationship to HIM--the Person, Truth.)

<u>Truth matters! And, in all matters, TRUTH!</u>

Unfortunately that statement doesn't seem to apply to 'global warming' or 'climate change,' in politics, government, academia, social conversation or, now apparently, in an Encyclical related to 'global warming' and 'climate change.' As mentioned in Chapter 2, I have included my pre-Laudato Si' position in Appendix A regarding 'global warming,' so it is not necessary to reargue the points, or to belabor further. If science does not pursue truth, then it isn't science. Therefore, I find it especially troubling to have an Encyclical setting forth, as truth, an alleged 'consensus' of scientists. Especially concerning are the reasons for settling for less than Truth. The world does not know Truth, and does not want to know Truth. Rather, it wants to do what it wants to do, and so it always has, from the very beginning, in the Garden of Eden.

The prototypical response of an unanchored world can (and does) accept all manner of sin because it does not know and does not want to know Truth Himself. The world grabs onto the word 'love' easily enough, but cannot live 'love' when it is based on lies. It is reminiscent of God's words to the Prophet Samuel in 1 Samuel 8:7: ***"… they have not rejected you, but they have rejected Me from being king over them."*** We cannot accept untruths and half-truths without at the same time rejecting Christ, the Truth, as King. There is an interesting juxtaposition to the verse from Samuel that may be found in Luke 19:27, verses which are not usually preached together.

Rio and a model for accepting half-truths

An Encyclical section which is especially disturbing is one regarding commitment to Truth. For all the avowal of a 'global warming' reality, Laudato Si' reveals a compromise on truth:

"The Rio Declaration of 1992 states that 'where there are threats of serious or irreversible damage, lack of full scientific certainty shall not be used as a pretext for postponing cost-effective measures' which prevent environmental degradation. This precautionary principle makes it possible to protect those who are most vulnerable and whose ability to defend their interests and to assemble incontrovertible evidence is limited." (#186)

Laudato Si' continues: *"The 1992 Earth Summit in Rio de Janeiro ... was a real step forward ... [but] ... poorly implemented due to the lack of suitable mechanisms for oversight, periodic review and penalties in cases of non-compliance. The principles which it proclaimed still await an efficient and flexible means of practical implementation." (#167)*

Furthermore, the impracticality of the Earth Summit's conclusion, as recounted above, is still a stumbling block to implementation regardless of what paper agreements may be executed.

It is troubling that the words from a conference in Rio held 23 years ago (and basically not implementable) should be an Encyclical argument today, and be a standard against which to justify a macroeconomic project driven by unproven 'global warming' and 'climate change' allegations -- a project which, once undertaken, will be difficult to ever stop and will burden all sectors of society, including the poor, who are likely to lose some resources. The issue isn't about making judgments on less than full information, but rather avowing the 'truth' of 'global warming' and 'climate change,' which lack proof but anecdotally drive public opinion, which also is not science.

It is one thing to evaluate an invasive project in the environment (dam building, fracking, harvesting nearly extinct species) and require it to present for approval the dangers and safety issues with which it would be associated. It is far different to make a worldwide pronouncement, invading rights of individuals and sovereign states, using up enormous financial resources, without proof of its necessity, or its anticipated efficacy.

Of course it is quite reasonable that proponents of a project should have to justify the safety of a project before undertaking it. This is not just a theoretical issue; closer to home in the Finger Lakes Region of New York State, there is the issue of fracking, with sincere people on both sides of the issue, one side oriented to the economy, and one side to protection of water supplies and the environment. And we consider the additional argument that even if a project CAN be done safely, it does not mean that we can trust that it WILL be done safely, as numerous failures have shown, especially:

- the EPA release of mine sludge, destroying the Animas River in Colorado,
- the prolonged BP oil well spill in the Gulf of Mexico, and
- the tragic Exxon Valdez oil spill destroying pristine Alaskan shoreline.

Pope Francis states well the concerns of many regarding fracking, when he writes: *"...some questions must have higher priority ... water is a scarce and indispensable resource, and a fundamental right which conditions the exercise of other human rights. This indisputable fact overrides any other assessment of environmental impact on a region."* (#185) In my opinion, we ought to be able to agree that water availability is not the same as many other resources, and so does deserve a special level of attention.

That the now 23-year-old ineffective and insufficient conclusions from Rio are still being quoted, as if worth recommendation, lends particular concern regarding the likely staying power of an Encyclical which has some of the problems we are discussing in this monograph, keeping alive obsolete wishes, and subject to misinterpretation or misuse.

Geocentrism again?

It has been shocking how quickly and thoroughly the Encyclical supported such spurious and grossly unproven theories as 'climate change,' without even the most minor challenge to the premises, references to counterarguments, or caution to the lemmings. It was reminiscent of Pope Urban VIII's enthusiastic embrace of geocentrism, obviously without sufficient evidence to have done so, and we've been hearing about it ever since, much to the prolonged shame and embarrassment of the Catholic Church. One might even come to ask if Laudato Si' isn't, in its own evangelism, a new kind of geocentrism. Such is the risk of meddling influence outside the areas of one's authority and expertise.

Consensus cannot manufacture Truth

Truth does not depend on consensus, nor is it created by human opinion. It is a shame that Laudato Si' even uses such a justification.   There is a relevant, popular quote credited to a number of religious personages, including Venerable Fulton J. Sheen, although no attribution is quite certain: "The truth is the truth even if nobody believes it, and error is error even if everybody believes it." It is an excellent argument as to why consensus doesn't matter. (Being strong against 'consensus justification' will be a crucial ability when persecution descends, and we refuse to put a single grain of incense on the coals to worship in 'One World Religion.')

Since we are not dealing with a claim of 'private revelation' or infallibility in Laudato Si', it seems fair to read the Encyclical at face value, beginning with the introductory comment:

"I will begin by briefly reviewing several aspects of the present ecological crisis, with the aim of drawing on the results of the best scientific research available today, letting them touch us deeply and provide a concrete foundation for the ethical and spiritual itinerary that follows." (#15)

Those words, "*The best scientific research available today,*" may claim to be the 'best' research but, unfortunately, it is not nearly adequate! A bad foundation is worse than no foundation; i.e. it is better not to know something, than to 'know' an untruth. If there were merit to 'global warming' or to 'climate change,' those claims ought to offer defense against the scientists who have put their names and reputations on the line to argue against the popular rhetoric. (See authors in Appendix C). Moreover, those who stake out the global-warming position have even failed to present the kind of credible analysis from which one could derive how much 'action' is necessary for what level of results. Or how success will be measured. Thus, the content is weak and compromised.

It is still not clear if 'climate change' means it might change, so let's prevent it, or it has already changed, so let's change it back. It seems to often mean 'just *do* something!' Separated from Truth, it means whatever the speaker or writer wants it to mean. There is a glaring lack of footnote information on which to lay a scientific basis and proof, leaving the avowals as mere opinion, not fact. Appendix C references raise further doubt. Here are further quotes from Laudato Si' in support of the unproven hypotheses of 'global warming:'

"A very solid scientific consensus indicates that we are presently witnessing a disturbing warming of the climatic system." (*#23*) No scientific references.

"...this warming has been accompanied by a constant rise in the sea level and, it would appear, by an increase of extreme weather events, even if a scientifically determinable cause cannot be assigned to each particular phenomenon." (*#23*) No scientific references.

"It is true that there are other factors (such as volcanic activity, variations in the earth's orbit and axis, the

solar cycle), yet a number of scientific studies indicate that most global warming in recent decades is due to the great concentration of greenhouse gases ... released mainly as a result of human activity." (#23) There are no references to these so-called 'scientific studies,' or to analysis of other significant variables.

"Climate change is a global problem with grave implications .... Its worst impact will probably be felt by developing countries in coming decades." (#25) *"Probably?"* What definitive conclusion is that, upon which to launch expensive global actions, still challenged by experts?

"There has been a tragic rise in the number of migrants seeking to flee from the growing poverty caused by environmental degradation." (#25) Where is documentation of the numbers of migrants vs. causes of migration; e.g. what percentage is due to religious persecution? No scientific or media references are given for substantiation.

Using words like *"it would appear,"* and *"probably be felt"* weakens any assertion of scientific Truth, as does the absence of supporting footnotes or refutation of publications by thoughtful scientists disagreeing with the claim of 'global warming.' (See Appendix C.)

The eventual fallout:

One of the worst effects of an Encyclical's claiming that 'global warming' and 'climate change' are 'true' is the perception by both the faithful and by others that the Catholic Church is 'teaching' such pseudo-science, risking loss of trust in doctrinal teaching, and creating an unnecessary stumbling block to evangelization.

<u>**Reflection**</u>

When God is turned away from His rightful place among a people, such as in schools, public events and discourse, and when what is most reprehensible to God is encouraged to prevail, it is no wonder that the people don't immediately recognize the Hand of God at work in climate and weather. Rather, they more quickly see their own hands at work, whether causing a problem of pollution or in the expectation of their own capabilities to relieve such problems.

In earlier generations, it was quite reasonable to pray, privately and publicly, for good weather and the bounty of crops, and to offer thanksgiving when so blessed. Today, it is uncommon to read in the media or to hear news announcers even mention the name of God, whether in the context of volcano, earthquake, tsunami, hurricane or tornado, although insurance companies still exempt 'acts of God' from their coverage. There is almost an embarrassed silence when trapped miners who have prayed for rescue are raised to the surface and drop to their knees.

Is it any wonder, then, when the adverse and unexpected occurs, that God is not 'top of mind,' but rather that criticism of other humans, including the government, plays out, as in hurricane Katrina?   When the larger context is missed, any explanation will do. Yet, it is worthwhile seriously pondering St. Paul's words in Hebrews, Chapter 1, verses 10-12:

"...Thou, Lord, didst found the earth in the beginning, and the heavens are the work of Thy hands; they will perish, but Thou remainest; they will all grow old like a garment, like a mantle Thou wilt roll them up, and they will be changed. But Thou art the same, and Thy years will never end."

Chapter VII
<u>Truth is not the Enemy</u>

Chapter 3 of the Laudato Si' Encyclical is a very disappointing diatribe against science and technology, innocuously titled: "The human roots of the ecological crisis." One hardly knows, as either a scientist or a logician, how to respond to such an apparent contradiction to the roots and the success of the scientific method.

The Catholic Church can certainly argue that many of its members have played leading roles in developing and accelerating the scientific and experimental method and its breakthroughs. It is beyond our scope here to identify the plethora of Catholic scientists who should be on the list of contributors, but it is clear that a single misstep in how the Church treats scientific truth (Galileo affair) demeans the work of all scientists, and the Faith and Reason foundation to the Catholic Church.

<u>Faith and reason are compatible</u>

Fortunately, we have the work of Pope Saint John Paul II in *Fides et Ratio* (Ref. E-5), stating:

"Faith and reason are like two wings on which the human spirit rises to the contemplation of truth; and God has placed in the human heart a desire to know the truth—in a word, to know himself—so that, by knowing and loving God, men and women may also come to the fullness of truth about themselves."

The key message of that encyclical is that faith and reason are compatible and essential together. Pope Saint John Paul II warns that Faith without reason leads to superstition, but he also says that reason without faith leads to relativism and to nihilism, which we so sadly see today.

<u>Attacks on science and technology</u>

Laudato Si' challenges science: *"The basic problem ... is the way that humanity has taken up technology and its development according to an undifferentiated and one-dimensional paradigm ... [which] exalts the concept of a subject who, using logical and rational procedures, progressively approaches and gains control over an external object. This subject makes every effort to establish the scientific and experimental method, which in itself is already a technique of possession, mastery and transformation ... as if the subject were to find itself in the presence of something formless, completely open to manipulation." (#106)*

Upon reading these words, I simply wrote the very unscientific, emotional word "YIKES!" in the margin, when I perceived an almost total lack of respect for even scientific and technological fundamentals. Throwing out the value of centuries of the scientific method is illogical and untenable, as if it were the cause of people's going astray, rather than merely used as an instrument of human greed and sinfulness. It would be like throwing away apple growing because that 'might' have been the fruit eaten by Adam and Eve.

Laudato Si' continues: *"...many problems of today's world stem from the tendency ... to make the method and aims of science and technology an epistemological paradigm which shapes the lives of individuals and the workings of society. The effects of imposing this model on reality as a whole, human and social, are seen in the deterioration of the environment, but this is just one sign of a reductionism which affects every aspect of human and social life. We have to accept that technological products are not neutral ...."* (#107) We do not *"have to accept"* anything which is untrue, and pressure to do so is unwelcome.

"The technological paradigm has become so dominant that it would be difficult to do without its resources and even more difficult to utilize them without being dominated by their internal logic .... Technology tends to absorb everything into its ironclad logic, and those who are surrounded with technology 'know full well that it moves forward in the final analysis neither for profit nor for the well-being of the human race,' that 'in the most radical sense of the term power is its motive – a lordship over all.' ... Our capacity to make decisions, a more genuine freedom and the space for each one's alternative creativity are diminished." (#108) Space for my "*alternative creativity?*" What can this possibly mean, and how can there be any internal contradiction?

Whether or not science is used for protection, power, politics or profit is not inherent in science, but in the morals and values of the people who use it.

Anthropomorphic Allegations?

And, so, science and technology seem to have become the enemy, an enemy with alleged motives! Whether that is because of hatred or fear, or because those who are untrained are completely baffled or afraid, is hard to say. Absent from almost all the Laudato Si' writing is even a head nod to many scientific breakthroughs which have made the world decisively better and safer for so many people.

In its condemnation of the throwaway culture (let us hope science isn't becoming one of the throwaways), Laudato Si' does not even acknowledge that disposables have been key to infection control. The 'throwaway culture,' which is so denounced in Laudato Si', is largely responsible for modernizing health care procedures with single-use needles, unit doses and sterilization of plastics, which significantly have reduced mortality by minimizing cross-contamination risk. There is even a role for a 'throwaway culture' when carefully examined, but it is as if we should get rid of matches, because some people die in fires, or get rid of all plastic which doesn't biodegrade, or all weapons because they allegedly 'cause wars,' or all art and illustration because it might lead to pornography!

These particular points are among the most illogical in Laudato Si', and a true embarrassment to Catholics who are grateful for their God-given abilities in science and technology and for the many accomplishments wrought through God's gifts to humans. In spite of this apparent aversion to science and technology, the irony is that Laudato Si' seems more than willing to appropriate the arguments of 'consensus' scientists, even though unproven, for the purpose of promulgating theories of 'global warming' and 'climate control.'

Moreover, there is an issue of tone, as if somehow science and technology were evil cousins. The Encyclical reads as if science and technology have a willful existence per se, like HAL, the singularity-driven computer in the movie "2001: A Space Odyssey."

The independence which most matters to scientists, and hence to science, is TRUTH. One cannot wish a disease to go away on its own, or deliver water without relatively high-pressure conduits and adequate treatment systems, or communicate globally, real-time, without satellites and high-speed devices. These technologies themselves do not contaminate the world and put it at risk. Rather, people of unformed conscience, abusers and exploiters, who misuse the technologies, are the problem. For Christ said:

"Do you not see that whatever goes into the mouth passes into the stomach and so passes on? But what comes out of the

mouth proceeds from the heart, and this defiles a man. For out of the heart come evil thoughts, murder, adultery, fornication, theft, false witness, slander. These are what defile a man; but to eat with unwashed hands does not defile a man." (Matthew 15:17-20) So, too, science and technology do not defile; rather, it is how they are used.

The Church as voice to the world

Shocking, therefore, are the sad words of Laudato Si':

"Nor are there genuine ethical horizons to which one can appeal." (#110) Isn't the Catholic Church supposed to provide this role to the world, even at the risk of unpopularity, and do so with leadership and persistence, not simply to mimic the words of other world powers? Not to throw in her lot with those of such myopic vision? Is she not the true "genuine ethical horizon?" Perhaps it is just such misunderstanding that is a foundation to the call for a secular super-power committee to rule? (See Chapter X.)

The Church cannot effectively aid the world to make the best use of our abilities and gifts by merely condemning the tools of progress. That would lead to failure in her mission. And, calling that very mission to mind, inevitably raises the question of how such condemnation, of science and technology, aids the mission to: *"Go therefore and make disciples of all nations, baptizing them in the Name of the Father and of the Son and of the Holy Spirit, teaching them to observe all that I have commanded you; and lo, I am with you always, to the close of the age."* (Matthew 28:19-20)

What can possibly be antithetical to our mission from science and technology? Have science and technology outpaced human kind? Or has the human race fallen short of keeping up with Truth, and witnessing to the Word, which cannot be hidden? The answers are to be found in the soul, not in the gene, the byte or the atom. I fear this orientation against science and technology will only delay true evangelization of souls, and place a stumbling block in their paths. We return to this subject in Chapter XIV regarding the Church's role.

Cultural Revolution, babies and bath water

Laudato Si' calls for a *"bold cultural revolution"* (#114) These words seem reminiscent of the Communist use of young people to enforce Mao's beliefs in China, to destroy what was good, to create a bleak landscape. It was called a "cultural revolution," and its damage has persisted for many decades. Such words in Laudato Si' about science and technology are similar to what was said about art, theater, writing and culture during the reign of the Red Guard.

There is radicalism about such a call that can lead to much wider destruction, and throwing out the very good which should be saved, but saving what is evil or perverse. We have been warned. Continuing to see technology blamed is reminiscent of the Red Guard's reign in China because people were pulled away from their heritage, especially by those who wanted to control and manipulate. It was class warfare, and ageist, and took away a basis of endurance and resistance.

Stop the world, I want to get off?

Are we now to abandon the basics of the scientific method, in order to slow down to n^{th}-world progress? It seems that might be the point. We catch a glimpse that Pope Francis would like the developed world to slow down, to turn back the clock and give the nth-world time to catch up! The dilemma is how to even have a rational conversation on the subject, let alone to consider who would be the decision makers. But we should note these words carefully:

"Nobody is suggesting a return to the Stone Age, but we do need to slow down and look at reality in a different way." (#114)

"...given the insatiable and irresponsible growth produced over many decades, we need also to think of containing growth by setting some reasonable limits and even retracing our steps before it is too late." (#193)

"...the time has come to accept decreased growth in some parts of the world, in order to provide resources for other places to experience healthy growth." (#193)

The socialistic aspects of Laudato Si' will be dealt with further in Chapter X; however, we first look at the question of whether or not those proposals are a cover for coveting?

Global coveting?

To slow down one economy on the theory that another could speed up is indeed collectivist, and has no relevant example of successful implementation on any scale, even in holding back high-achieving children for the benefits of their classmates' self-esteem. As almost any business understands, what works at a small, experimental level in the laboratory often cannot be scaled up, at least not without a lot of re-engineering. Its weaknesses are magnified during scale-up, sometimes to the point of impossibility. So too have been most social experiments which impinge free will.

To seize or to hamstring what is most productive in one sector will ultimately attack both human rights and property rights in all sectors, stymieing greed in one but stimulating covetousness in the other, a mere transfer of vices. It would be like having half a nation on food stamps and expecting the other half to work harder, being naïve about human motivation as both halves devolve. It fosters resentment and erodes charity.

That is not to say there are no inequalities; but the greater need is to evangelize souls to charity, to a change of heart, rather than locking up or impairing the gifts God has given them all. If we do not believe that is possible, do we have any right to preach to the world in His Name?

Unfortunately, the Encyclical is rife with implications of violations of the Tenth Commandment, of taking from the work of one and giving to another. Worse than infringing the rights of the one who is mugged in the process, is the taking away of that person's ability to freely give what he or she no longer has, of stripping the ability of the individual to grow into a benevolence of heart.

Are 'global warming' and alleged 'climate change' being used for another agenda, one for which Truth seems unimportant? An agenda which encourages covetousness and transplants greed? An agenda which foments dissatisfaction to the benefit of a 'new world' leadership? An agenda which inevitably transitions to class warfare?

One King

There is only one king, Christ the King, and all other efforts are subversive and covetous. The Tenth Commandment states ***"Thou shalt not covet ... anything that is your neighbor's."*** (Exodus 20:17) What else is being coveted in the exhortations of Laudato Si'?

Coveting control of science?

Laudato Si' states:

"...it is essential to give researchers their due role, to facilitate their interaction, and to ensure broad academic freedom." (#140)

Here is a disconnect to how researchers really work. Scientists are perfectly capable of facilitating their own interactions without government intrusion. But, today, most researchers trying to argue against 'global warming' or 'climate change' can hardly experience 'broad academic freedom.' They have little chance, for example, to secure adequate funding for research which is oriented to disproving 'global warming.'

Further interference in the process will ensure less true science, not more. One also has to be careful to allow researchers to develop their appropriate roles without Big Brother's peering over their shoulders. 'Facilitate' sounds a lot like 'control,' as in facilitating a two-year old to cross the street by holding his or her hand. Or having scientists control each other's work?

Coveting what resources?

"...since the effects of climate change will be felt for a long time to come, even if stringent measures are taken now, some countries ... will require assistance ...." (#170)

A reasonable question is, since no scientific data are cited, and no reference upon which the above excerpt depends, how then can anyone reach the conclusion that *"the effects of climate change will be felt for a long time to come"*? This is the very kind of assertion which science and technology reasonably challenge, and which perhaps makes the climate change people very uncomfortable.

Further, Laudato Si' does not specify what those resources are, or what *'some countries'* might be. The danger is that when resources are later determined (or later revealed if they are already determined) it will be claimed that the Encyclical already had called for those resources, when the very ambiguity of the words makes such call ineffective. But that is what comes from embracing what is not proven, from what is not based on data and analysis and from not revealing all the information in a timely manner.

Coveting financial resources?

'Follow the money' is a popular expression. But Robin Hood type cash flow is not a measure of righteousness or charity. Regarding so-called 'climate change,' we don't know if it's real, how it's caused, or what is its likely trajectory, but there is surety that it will be *"felt for a long time to come?"* (#170)

On the other hand, an almost throwaway sentence in paragraph #168, points out something which seems not to have received much attention: the resilience of nature.

"Thanks to the Vienna Convention for the protection of the ozone layer and its implementation through the Montreal Protocol and amendments, the [ozone] layer's thinning seems to have entered a phase of resolution." (#168)

Who knew that what was so often reported as a damaged ozone layer, expected to persist for centuries, is being resolved? Why don't we know that, and does it indicate a resiliency in nature that some don't want to admit? Is there a program and funding for that purpose now in place that can be terminated and the funds applied elsewhere? Does it bode well for resolving 'global warming,' if it exists now? And are the claims of persisting *"for a long time to come"* grossly exaggerated for the sense of pushing program implementation? Or just a guess? A threat? Is it principally a financial strategy to move funds from wealthier to less wealthy nations? Is it just driven by a desire for re-allocation of wealth? Who will measure the cash flow and report against what targets? Which country's accounting system will be used? What percentage of any funds actually transferred will be distributed, versus retained at government levels? Will any distributions be mandated for infrastructure, or will distributions be windfall bonus payments to current citizens, and a 'slush fund' for shaky governments?

Coveting Power?

One does get the impression that the coveting is being done far more by a high 'controlling' authority than by the victims of their own covetous leaders. Moreover, if the leaders of the recipient countries can't be trusted today to administer their responsibilities well, what is the likelihood that they will be more dependable with more of other countries' money?

Finance, politics and power (and their derivative words) are used frequently throughout Laudato Si'. These are not the key words with which the Catholic Church is principally concerned in her preaching the Gospel of Jesus Christ. It is one of the great temptations, to rule rather than serve. Thus, Jesus felt it necessary, shortly before He died, to give a specific warning, a warning which is also a test of obedience to Him, in Matthew 20:25-28:

"But Jesus called them to Him and said, "You know that the rulers of the Gentiles lord it over them, and their great men exercise authority over them. It shall not be so among you; but whoever would be great among you must be your servant, and whoever would be first among you must be your slave; even as the Son of man came not to be served but to serve, and to give His life as a ransom for many."

See also Luke 22:25-26.

I find it hard to see the evidence of this teaching in the following 'power' quotes of Laudato Si'. There are 56 which refer to power, and 19 to powerful. Here is a sampling:

"...the new power structures based on the techno-economic paradigm may overwhelm not only our politics but also freedom and justice." (#53)

"...economic powers continue to justify the current global system where priority tends to be given to speculation and the pursuit of financial gain ...." (#56)

"...Judaeo-Christian thought demythologized nature ... it no longer saw nature as divine ... emphasizes all the more our human responsibility for nature. A fragile world ... challenges us to devise intelligent ways of directing, developing and limiting our power." (#78) Clearly this triumph of Judaeo-Christian thought in 'demythologizing' nature is in danger of being lost.

"...since resources end up in the hands of the first comer or the most powerful: the winner takes all." (#82)

"...many other abilities which we have acquired ... have given us tremendous power .... Never has humanity had such power over itself, yet nothing ensures that it will be used wisely. ... In whose hands does all this power lie, or will it eventually end up? It is extremely risky for a small part of humanity to have it." (#104) It is also risky for every part of humanity to have the same access, as nuclear powers in Iran's hands may well demonstrate.

"The fact is that 'contemporary man has not been trained to use power well' ... 'the risk is growing day by day that man will not use his power as he should' ... 'power is never considered in terms of the responsibility of choice which is inherent in freedom' since its 'only

norms are taken from alleged necessity, from either utility or security' .... [W]e stand naked and exposed in the face of our ever-increasing power, lacking the wherewithal to control it." (#105)

"...in the most radical sense of the term power is its motive - a lordship over all." (#108)

"...cult of unlimited human power ...." (#122)

"...restraints occasionally have to be imposed on those possessing greater resources and financial power ...." (#129)

"...a technology severed from ethics will not easily be able to limit its own power." (#136)

"...governments are reluctant to upset the public with measures which could affect the level of consumption or create risks for foreign investment. The myopia of power politics delays the inclusion of a far-sighted environmental agenda within the overall agenda of governments." (#178)

"Unless citizens control political power - national, regional and municipal - it will not be possible to control damage to the environment." (#179)

There is a naïveté regarding how much of a difference a 'citizen vote' would make in the environment. The current U.S. situation shows that individuals are not above voting themselves money and license to sin, as chief priorities. The experiment of democracy, which has always depended on following a higher law, fails when that Higher Law Giver is repudiated.

"Saving banks at any cost ... only reaffirms the absolute power of a financial system, a power which has no future and will only give rise to new crises, after a slow, costly and only apparent recovery." (#189)

"...subsidiarity ... demand[s] a greater sense of responsibility for the common good from those who wield greater power." (#196)

"...those really free are the minority who wield economic and financial power ... (#203) This is perhaps one of the more difficult assertions to understand, since the 'really free' would seem to be those who have put everything in God's hands.

"A change in lifestyle could bring healthy pressure to bear on those who wield political, economic and social power." (#206) This two-edged sword begs the question of what kind of power is exerted against sin and sinful lifestyles?

Laudato Si' rightly states: *"Honesty and truth are needed in scientific and political discussions."* (#183) Too bad we haven't seen that evidence with respect to the unscientific seizure of 'global warming' and 'climate change' rhetoric, by a vast number of would-be policy makers and influencers, who ignore Truth and covet what others have.

Truth is inviolable, particularly when it is expected from religious leaders; people are especially vulnerable to the forces they exert, and the thoughts and emotions they influence. Religious leaders will not be trusted with spiritual truth if not trustworthy regarding material truth. And that is the real danger of choosing sides regarding unproven issues and either exerting influence beyond the sphere of faith or misusing power within the sphere of faith.

Chapter VIII

<u>Sustainability</u>

A code word which the United Nations and its liberal affiliates and supporters often use is 'sustainability.' Apparently it means whatever the speaker wants it to mean, at that time. Some advocates express an extreme goal of reducing the world population from seven billion to one billion people for the sake of the earth, which is, de facto, a kind of pantheistic sacrifice.

<u>Sustainability clearly means population reduction</u>

How is such reduction of population likely to be accomplished? War, diseases like Ebola (where did it go? was it just a test case for managing global spread? For developing vaccines?), and plague all have their part in reducing population. Hitler advocated genocide, as the 'final solution,' killing Jews, priests, disabled, impaired, young and elderly. On the near horizon is persecution of Christians, by designating 'truth' a form of terrorism.

There has even been a movement reported in Europe to kill ('euthanize') children up to 2 years old. One campaign recently sought to euthanize up to 12 years old. At the other end of life is legalizing heirs to approve euthanizing their parents. There was a time when such thoughts may never have entered our consciousness or, if they did, we were sure none of these atrocities could ever take root in the United States. Sadly, now it is generally believed we will escape none of these threats. Further, the rate of incursion of such sin is accelerating demonically to speeds which heretofore would have seemed impossible.

Such wild imaginings are only dwarfed by the 'wilder' positions of sustainability. Laudato Si' uses sustainability words 27x (sustainable 19x; sustainability 2x; unsustainable 3x; sustain, sustains and sustained 1x each), creating the appearance of cooperation with a global agenda which can never be compromised or fit into Catholic Teaching. Rather, the opportunity has been missed to teach strongly against the principles of sustainability, just as it was missed 40+ years ago to take a proactive stand against abortion in the United States.

Global Pressure for Sustainability

The sustainability advocates have brought pressure on the Vatican, through the United Nations, to permit contraceptives and abortions in n^{th}-world countries, and threatened charges of 'torture' against the Catholic Church for its teaching on abortion and homosexuality. A prominent newspaper once called Pope Francis 'cruel' for (rightly) calling abortion a 'sin.'

Other financial pressures are used on sovereign nations, like African countries, to try to force them to support abortion and same-sex unions. 'Funding for compliance' it might be called. There have also been recent rumors, still not fully documented, but credible and timely, that a tetanus vaccine sent to Kenya may have contained ingredients which prevent women from bearing children. The number and frequency of such charges depict a mindset and a fear that is noteworthy, even when proof of individual allegations is still being researched. It is a logical carryover from the work of Margaret Sanger, who sought to disproportionately abort babies of color.

In Canada and the United States, government has increasingly seized public education to advance its own agenda, beginning with shaping the sexuality of very young children, to developing children who are blind to evil and inured to institutionalized sin. Sustainability of the earth becomes the argument, or at least a code word for the argument, reflecting a profound lack of trust in the God Who created humankind and the earth, and said: ***"Be fruitful and multiply."*** (Genesis 1:22, 28) The stakes are enormous; it is about souls, not about environmental pollution or the social agenda.

Code Words and the United Nations

The code word 'sustainability' is sprinkled throughout Laudato Si'; it is the death rattle of sabers in the closet and hobnail boots in the Sanctuary. One cannot avoid the conclusion that the choice of the mild word-stem 'sustain' is deliberate (just as 'choice' was for abortion), and it seems like one more point of serious confusion for Catholics. It would have been, in my opinion, far more preferable for Laudato Si' to have used a different word, to clearly separate what the Catholic Church believes from the sinful agenda of the United Nations and its affiliate programs and conferences. And it would have been far more preferable for Laudato Si' to have used the teaching opportunity to denounce the program and elements of sustainability. Its silence in teaching the Faith by preaching such truth is the greater disappointment. A broader question is whether or not the failure to denounce sustainability strategy clearly is, in its essence, also misleading the world?

Influence of international conferences and organizations

Many footnotes in Laudato Si' reference international conferences with goals to which the Encyclical implicitly aligns itself. Some conferences are bishops' conferences, others of a more secular nature. Although it is not articulated that Catholics are obligated to agree with all the output of those conferences, the focus nonetheless suggests some support.

For those who don't know about the United Nations' sustainability goals, a primer can be found at some of the websites listed in Appendix F. There are four conferences which shed some light on the text of Laudato Si':

a. <u>Istanbul:</u>   Of concern in the Encyclical is footnote #18, which references *"Global Responsibility and Ecological Sustainability,"* closing remarks from the Halki Summit I, Istanbul, June 2012. We are presented with no explanation or credible argument as to why such theories outside the Catholic Church should form a basis to teach any version of sustainability in an Encyclical, or why Catholics would, in conscience, ever be able to support the full agenda of the United Nations.

b. <u>Rio:</u> One can also read the 26 page Rio report referenced in Laudato Si' (dated 2010 but covering through conferences in 2012.) Even a quick perusal shows similar language and mindsets to Laudato Si'. One might question having an Encyclical of the Catholic Church depend on secular and pseudo-government propaganda.

Laudato Si' states: *"The 1992 Earth Summit in Rio de Janeiro ... proclaimed that 'human beings are at the centre of concerns for sustainable development.'"* (#167) This statement is ambiguous, as it can mean the reduction in number of human beings, or reduction in their reproduction, almost always through immoral practices, or it can simply mean it will take human beings to solve global problems. Generally, it is not useful to recount the ambiguous, except in cases where the ambiguous could be a deliberate cover by secular forces for that which cannot be morally articulated now, but which risks being conveniently reinterpreted at some future point. Ambiguity in this important arena is dangerous.

c. <u>The Hague:</u> "The Earth Charter" formulated in The Hague in 2000 is yet another one of the documents underlying the Encyclical and referenced in it.

d. <u>Aparecida, Brazil:</u> The Aparecida Conference, which is quoted twice in Laudato Si', is of particular interest because

Jorge Cardinal Bergoglio (now Pope Francis) not only attended this Fifth Latin American Episcopal Conference held in May, 2007 in Aparecida, Brazil, but also was elected to chair the committee charged with drafting the final document. (Ref. E-6) Thus, it becomes of some interest to find any foreshadowing of environmental concerns regarding the Encyclical or its implementation in a text written eight years earlier.

The quotes below are from the Aparecida Concluding Document, which is quite an impressive piece of work. The tone is measured, precise, and relatively thorough, quite different from Laudato Si'. Similar subjects were undertaken in the two documents, but Aparecida relates the environmental issues more closely to words of faith, with a more gentle tone:

- "…we call on all living forces of society to take care of our common house, the earth threatened of destruction. We want to favor a human and sustainable development based upon a just distribution of wealth and the communion of goods among all peoples." Message of the Fifth General Conference to the Peoples of Latin America and the Caribbean, Paragraph 4.

- "Preserving nature is very often subordinated to economic development, with damage to biodiversity, exhaustion of water reserves and other natural resources, air pollution, and climate change." Paragraph 66, Concluding Document.

- "Latin America has the most abundant aquifers on the planet, along with vast extensions of forest lands which are humanity's lungs. The world thus receives free of charge environmental services, benefits that are not recognized economically." Paragraph 66. (This point may be a claim in the future, but, it is not raised in the Encyclical regarding any alleged 'debt' of the Northern to the Southern Hemisphere.)

- "When truth, good, and beauty are separated, and when human persons and their fundamental exigencies do not constitute … ethical criterion, science and technology turn against the human being who has created them." Paragraph 123. (A bit of the anthropomorphic attribution to science and technology in Laudato Si' also occurs in this paragraph.)

- "Particular importance must be given to the most serious destruction under way in human ecology." Paragraph 472.

- "Today the natural wealth of Latin America and the Caribbean is being subjected to an irrational exploitation that is leaving ruin and even death in its wake ... attributed to the current economic model which prizes unfettered pursuit of riches over the life of individual persons and peoples and rational respect for nature. The devastation of our forests and biodiversity through a selfish predatory attitude, involves the moral responsibility of those who promote it ... jeopardizing ... millions of people ...." Paragraph 473.

- "...we must mention the problems caused by the savage uncontrolled industrialization of our cities and the countryside, which is polluting the environment with all kinds of organic and chemical wastes. A similar warning must be made about resource extraction industries which, when they fail to control and offset their harmful effects on the surrounding environment, destroy forests and contaminate water, and turn the areas exploited into vast deserts." Paragraph 473.

Laudato Si' and its direct support of sustainability

Laudato Si' states: *"...recent World Summits on the environment have not lived up to expectations because, due to lack of political will, they were unable to reach truly meaningful and effective global agreements on the environment." (#166)* There are reasons for lack of success, not always somebody else's failure. The inability to implement over many years says something about the likelihood of any ultimate success. The only strategy proposed, that of collectivist enforcement and forced 'payments,' is not logical.

A crucial quote in Laudato Si' is: *"Let ours be a time remembered for the awakening of a new reverence for life, the firm resolve to achieve sustainability, the quickening of the struggle for justice and peace, and the joyful celebration of life." (#207)*

One should not think that mere 'reverence for life' implies a pro-life position. Rather, even those people who favor radical sustainability actions reverence their own lives, and see their own lives as enhanced by the death of others.

Note particularly the words: *"...the firm resolve to achieve sustainability ...."* This kind of alignment to 'sustainability' jargon is a dangerous precedent, supportive of United Nations strategies, and open to reinterpretation in the future. Again, it seems that it would have been far preferable to have chosen a word better suited to Catholic Theology, and to have made a rallying position for all Catholics with just such language.

One gets the impression from these document references that Laudato Si' is not leading the way but rather is following the 'One World' route long ago plotted and lobbied, almost as if there were a different but parallel agenda.

Laudato Si' misses a major opportunity to more clearly condemn the practices recounted, such as pressure on African countries in particular and policies like China's "one child" program. One has to ask why these subjects are introduced and then the opportunity to teach is avoided, in an Encyclical explicitly said to be addressed to the world.

<u>Sustainability in related Encyclical excerpts</u>

The sustainability theme is unrelenting: *"The urgent challenge to protect our common home includes a concern to bring the whole human family together to seek a sustainable and integral development, for we know that things can change." (#13)*

"...the goals of this rapid and constant change are not necessarily geared to the common good or to integral and sustainable human development." (#18)

"...some can only propose a reduction in the birth rate ... [D]eveloping countries face forms of international pressure which make economic assistance contingent on certain policies of 'reproductive health' ... it is true that an unequal distribution of the population and of available resources creates obstacles to development and a sustainable use of the environment ...." (#50)

"There are regions now at high risk and, aside from all doomsday predictions, the present world system is certainly unsustainable from a number of points of view ...." (#61) What does this mean? What is unsustainable? People? Money? Technology? Education? Resources? Does this language not play right into the hands of those who argue overpopulation?

"...when we speak of 'sustainable use,' consideration must always be given to each ecosystem's regenerative ability in its different areas and aspects." (#140) However, continuing to read, we note there is no prescription to change what is railed against, no explanation how recommendations would be differentially applied to each ecosystem.

This point will be expanded in Chapter X in the analysis regarding the potential role of collectivism as a proposed solution. A desire for 'change' may be the motivator, but lack of disclosure understandably makes those on the receiving end of any impositions 'nervous.' What are the specific solutions to be imposed?

<u>**The financial aspect**</u>

Laudato Si' attacks waste in wealthier countries, a United Nations priority agenda item, which seeks ways to extricate funds from wealthier countries to support targeted causes.

We should not be surprised to find that there is more money involved than the words at first indicate. For example, there have been calls by the United Nations to make uniform lending and borrowing rates from first-world banks to n^{th}-world projects. That is antithetical to any banking system which, to have investors, must lend on the basis of return on capital employed, taking risk into account in the cost-of-capital equation. Otherwise, there will be no funds to lend unless a sovereign government de facto nationalizes the banks, or unless perhaps the Vatican is willing to provide the loans?

"...we need to grow in the conviction that a decrease in the pace of production and consumption can at times give rise to another form of progress and development .... Efforts to promote a sustainable use of natural resources are not a waste of money, but rather an investment capable of providing other economic benefits in the medium term ...." (#191) There is no suggestion as to how consumption can be decreased without getting rid of people or by strongly contracepting future generations. (Moreover, we do not *"need to grow"* in any *"conviction"* which is not true.)

The previous quotation seems to be somewhat disjointed from what follows: *"...talk of sustainable growth usually becomes a way of distracting attention and offering excuses. It absorbs the language and values of ecology into the categories of finance and technocracy, and the social and environmental responsibility of businesses often gets reduced to a series of marketing and image-enhancing measures."* (#194) One wonders how the post-

Encyclical bathing of St. Peter's Basilica in a controversial environmental light show by the World Bank fits the cited criticism of reduced responsibility by *"marketing and image enhancing measures"* in Laudato Si'.

If the conflict between those two prior quotations is a proxy for sustainability being whatever the United Nations says it is, then it really *is* about power, supported by socialistic bias.

At what price sustainability?

From so much that has been written, it appears that the Church's alignment to the United Nations' sustainability arguments will ultimately put Catholics in a spiritually untenable bind. The language rests uncomfortably side-by-side with inconsistent or unacceptable implications such as:

- If we really accepted the concept of unsustainability, which is unproven, like 'global warming' and 'climate change,' how do we protect against the creep toward a "lesser-of-two-evils" argument?
- Is aiding the United Nations' objectives regarding environment and pollution also abetting their immoral strategies?
- Since the most crucial resource of a human being is time, a totally non-renewable resource, where and how do the activities demanded by saluting the 'sustainability flag' impinge on our greater spiritual duties?

The reader can see that language and vocabulary in the United Nations' quotes and in the Encyclical avoid obvious statements of either compatibility or incompatibility between goals of the United Nations, and the Teaching Office of the Church. But what is especially disappointing is that, given the ear of the world, there is no taking 'head-on' the refutation of the evil being foisted through those sustainability programs.

Chapter IX
The Principle of Subsidiarity

The Catholic Church strongly embraces the Principle of Subsidiarity. The Catechism of the Catholic Church (CCC) (Ref. E-7), in paragraphs 1883 through 1885, regarding subsidiarity, is excerpted as follows:

CCC 1883: "...Excessive intervention by the state can threaten personal freedom and initiative. The teaching of the Church has elaborated the principle of *subsidiarity*, according to which 'a community of a higher order should not interfere in the internal life of a community of a lower order, depriving the latter of its functions, but rather should support it in case of need and help to co-ordinate its activity with the activities of the rest of society, always with a view to the common good.'"

CCC 1884: "...The way God acts in governing the world, which bears witness to such great regard for human freedom, should inspire the wisdom of those who govern human communities. They should behave as ministers of divine providence."

CCC 1885: "The principle of subsidiarity is opposed to all forms of collectivism. It sets limits for state intervention. It aims at harmonizing the relationships between individuals and societies. It tends toward the establishment of true international order."

Lip service to subsidiarity

Unfortunately, Laudato Si' seems to give lip service to the principle of subsidiarity but then proceeds to seriously violate the principle in repeated appeals to solve the world's environmental and ecological 'problems' at a secular level of the highest order. The word 'subsidiarity' (emphasis added) only occurs twice in the 40,000+ word Encyclical:

"Underlying the principle of the common good is respect for the human person as such, endowed with basic and inalienable rights ordered to his or her integral development. It has also to do with the overall welfare of society and the development of a variety of intermediate groups, applying the principle of **subsidiarity**. Outstanding among those groups is the family as the basic cell of society. Finally the common good calls for social peace, the stability and security provided by a certain order which cannot be achieved without particular concern for distributive justice; whenever this is violated, violence always ensues. Society as a whole, and the state in particular, are obliged to defend and promote the common good." (#157)

"What happens with politics? Let us keep in mind the principle of **subsidiarity,** which grants freedom to develop the capabilities present at every level of society, while also demanding a greater sense of responsibility for the common good from those who wield greater power. Today, it is the case that some economic sectors exercise more power than states themselves. But economics without politics cannot be justified, since this would make it impossible to favour other ways of handling the various aspects of the present crisis. The mindset which leaves no room for sincere concern for the environment is the same mindset which lacks concern for the inclusion of the most vulnerable members of society. For 'the current model, with its emphasis on success and self-reliance, does not appear to favour an investment in efforts to help the slow, the weak or the less talented to find opportunities in life.'" (#196)

The quote with which the excerpt above ends is by Pope Francis quoting himself in the Apostolic Exhortation Evangelium Gaudium, November 24, 2013.

Not all the conclusions in paragraph #196 are defended or proved, in particular the claim *"economics without politics cannot be justified,"* and the claim that *"no ... concern for the environment is the same mindset which lacks concern for the most vulnerable members of society."* Again, the linkage between the poor and the environment is weak and unclear, and the syllogism is lacking in logic.

Further, and relating to paragraph #157, the obligation to practice the principle of subsidiarity is not inherently dependent on the just exercise of power by those at higher levels or on their conformance to distributive justice; the principle remains valid, regardless.

Losing the sense of subsidiarity

Quotations from Laudato Si' seem to shift away from the Principle of Subsidiarity, and rarely if ever return to justify recommended actions with even a test related to subsidiarity. Rather, the conclusions appear to advocate placing key world decisions in the hands of a type of centralized planning committee. It should be noted that paragraph #195 ends with the assertion:

"An instrumental way of reasoning, which provides a purely static analysis of realities in the service of present needs, is at work whether resources are allocated by the market or by state central planning." (#195)

Once again the language confounds, but seems to be asserting that free-market factors or central planning (so common to socialist states) are equivalent on their relevant bases. (This is of course not true; there is no comparison between the exercise of God-given free will and slavery to dictatorship, no matter how seemingly benevolent.) Thematic to this Encyclical (which will be expanded in later chapters) is a sense that much of humanity is not to be trusted with its free will regarding the environment. We should remember that even when we misuse or abuse the environment, God Himself is not stepping in to reverse our actions; He gives free will to us and it has its price – for us as well as for the environment. Perhaps there is more need for trust in these matters than there is to institute centralized human controls? See CCC 1884 above.

There is no evidence or proof given to justify the assertion of equivalency between resources allocated by the market (and human will) vs. central planning. But it is in this context that we can view the numerous assertions in Laudato Si' that decisions of worldwide import should be handled at a level which supersedes the rights of sovereign nations and de facto ignores subsidiarity. For most people in western cultures, who value freedom and self-determination, some Encyclical assertions likely appear socialistic. The Catechism is clear in paragraph CCC 1885: "The principle of subsidiarity is opposed to all forms of collectivism."

In Chapter X, many of the collectivist and socialist quotes from Laudato Si' will be recounted. But first it is important to consider how Church teaching stands on the shoulders of prior magisterial pronouncements, and how carefully one must approach excerpts.

Magisterial teaching on subsidiarity

In Chapter II it was mentioned that all the quotes in Laudato Si' would be taken at face value as being the words of Pope Francis, without attempting to dissect the quotes and their context and prior references. To this point, that has been true. But arriving at this section on subsidiarity, which should be an essential underpinning of any Catholic global teaching on environmentalism, pollution, alleged 'climate change' and imposition of penalties, it is absolutely necessary to first revisit the basis for the teaching, especially since Pope Francis uses quotes by other papal sources to justify or support his own.

We must remember that Popes do not simply appear, asserting teaching unconnected to all prior history but, rather, they are also the custodians of all prior magisterial teaching. They are protectors of doctrine. But when I was reading the following reference (#175) in Laudato Si' it did not ring true to me regarding either the Catechism paragraph CCC 1885, or Pope Benedict's own words in the Ratzinger Report (Ref. E-8). (See Chapter X.)

Hence, it was necessary to put aside, for this particular instance, the prior guideline that simply accepted all quotes at face value as belonging to Pope Francis, no matter who is cited. In this case, with a teaching expected to stand on the shoulders of prior papal teaching, it seemed vital to confirm what Pope Benedict is reported to have said. My own observations and interpretations of Pope Benedict's prior statements did not support the conclusion in Laudato Si'. I was only able to notice the apparent disconnect because of personal familiarity with and deep respect for the writings of Cardinal Ratzinger (i.e. Pope Benedict XVI).

<u>A problematic excerpt which misleads</u>

Laudato Si' states:

"...it is essential to devise stronger and more efficiently organized international institutions, with functionaries who are appointed fairly by agreement among national governments, and empowered to impose sanctions." (#175) Many people in more democratic societies would likely see these words as socialist or collectivist.

In defense of these words, Pope Francis immediately quotes in the same paragraph and very next sentence: *"As Benedict XVI has affirmed in continuity with the social teaching of the Church:"* and then there is an excerpted quote from Pope Benedict, from paragraph #67 of Caritas in Veritate (CiV), (Ref. E-9), reading as if the excerpt from Pope Benedict were a rousing endorsement of the text in Paragraph #175 of Laudato Si'.

This is the quote attributed to Pope Benedict: *'To manage the global economy; to revive economies hit by the crisis; to avoid any deterioration of the present crisis and the greater imbalances that would result; to bring about integral and timely disarmament, food security and peace; to guarantee the protection of the environment and to regulate migration: for all this, there is urgent need of a true world political authority, as my predecessor Blessed John XXIII indicated some years ago."* (#175)

While Pope Francis correctly attributes this quote to Pope Benedict, it is out of context, since essential language before and after the quote from Caritas in Veritate is omitted, i.e. language which contains important, mitigating factors, particularly the subsidiarity test (mentioned twice by Pope Benedict), a vital perspective in such matters.

Shown below is the same Laudato Si' excerpt, but with the remainder of paragraph #67 from Pope Benedict's Caritas in Veritate (CiV) shown in Arial grey bold on either side of the excerpt, with what had been expurgated now giving context.

Without that missing language, it seems that the Laudato Si' quote is easily misunderstood. (Underlining is added to draw attention to certain words and phrases significantly lost in excerpting from Pope Benedict's writing.) We cannot know if the language was dropped deliberately, or if it was misunderstood and considered irrelevant, or if it was simply a space need, but careful reading will show the missing text is quite important. (Note too that a key part of the context is Pope Benedict's call for reform of the United Nations, rather than simply seeing it as an organization to which authority should be given, or control surrendered, over the problems of the world.)

What Pope Benedict actually said in 2009 in CiV 67, which also quotes other prior sources (missing language is shown in Arial grey bold; emphasis added):

"In the face of the unrelenting growth of global interdependence, there is a strongly felt need, even in the midst of a global recession, for a reform of the United Nations Organization, and likewise of economic institutions and international finance, so that the concept of the family of nations can acquire real teeth. One also senses the urgent need to find innovative ways of implementing the principle of the responsibility to protect [146] and of giving poorer nations an effective voice in shared decision-making. This seems necessary in order to arrive at a political, juridical and economic order which can increase and give direction to international cooperation for the development of all peoples in solidarity. [Note that footnote 146 in CiV 67 is to a speech given to the General Assembly of the United Nations in 2008 (Ref. E-10).]

"To manage the global economy; to revive economies hit by the crisis; to avoid any deterioration of the present crisis and the greater imbalances that would result; to bring about integral and timely disarmament, food security and peace; to guarantee the protection of the environment and to regulate migration: for all this, there is urgent need of a true world political authority, as my predecessor Blessed John XXIII indicated some years ago." (#175)

Then Pope Benedict continued:

"Such an authority would need to be regulated by law, to observe consistently the principles of subsidiarity and solidarity, to seek to establish the common good *[147]*, and to make a commitment to securing authentic integral human development inspired by the values of charity in truth. Furthermore, such an authority would need to be universally recognized and to be vested with the effective power to ensure security for all, regard for justice, and respect for rights *[148]*. Obviously it would have to have the authority to ensure compliance with its decisions from all parties, and also with the coordinated measures adopted in various international forums. Without this, despite the great progress accomplished in various sectors, international law would risk being conditioned by the balance of power among the strongest nations. The integral development of peoples and international cooperation require the establishment of a greater degree of international ordering, marked by subsidiarity, for the management of globalization *[149]*. They also require the construction of a social order that at last conforms to the moral order, to the interconnection between moral and social spheres, and to the link between politics and the economic and civil spheres, as envisaged by the Charter of the United Nations."

Missing language

Notice the textual development in particular, jumping from *functionaries empowered to impose sanctions'* in Laudato Si' (#175) to continue in the very next sentence, same paragraph, *"As Benedict affirmed ...,"* to skip the relevant text regarding reform of the United Nations Organization and also of economic institutions and international finance, provide the quote from Pope Benedict out of context, and then skip the text which includes the two references to subsidiarity.

The remaining language which was omitted obviously contains important modifiers regarding the requirement "to observe consistently the principles of 'subsidiarity' and 'solidarity,' and values of charity in truth, regard for justice and respect for rights, and more. Pope Benedict also makes it clear (in his own words and in quoting others) that any such change would need to be "universally recognized," have regard for justice and rights, and a greater degree of international ordering, marked by subsidiarity. We note that the reform language directed toward the United Nations and both these references to subsidiarity were eliminated in the excerpt of Pope Benedict's words in paragraph #175 of Laudato Si'.

We should remember how precise Pope Emeritus Benedict XVI has always been in the formulation of his thoughts. One simply cannot eliminate qualifiers and modifiers in order to use his words to support 'subject-verb-object' conclusions. Without subsidiarity, the conclusions of the numerous quotes above are simply not Catholic conclusions. But is it socialism, marxism or some other brand of collectivism? Or something else? Those concerns are developed further in Chapter X.

NOTE: This quotation in Laudato Si' from Pope Benedict's address to the United Nations is the <u>only</u> instance in this monograph in which the original context was examined. Other attributions in the 172 footnotes of Laudato Si' are accepted herein as being Pope Francis' own words, with context unverified. Such verification is beyond the scope of this monograph, but the present significant disparity should alert scholars to examine footnotes more closely for both context and validation.

Chapter X
<u>Socialism? Liberation Theology?</u>

There is no better way to begin Chapter X than to continue with quotes from Pope Benedict XVI, as Cardinal Ratzinger, in <u>The Ratzinger Report</u>. It is as if he were looking decades into the future at some of the concerns we've been discussing. Note that the comments of the man who would be the future Pope Benedict XVI go well beyond the mere question of socialism.

"… the marxist [sic] ideology actually uses the Jewish-Christian tradition and turns it into a godless prophetic movement; man's religious energies are used as a tool for political ends and directed to a merely earthly hope, which is equivalent to standing on its head the Christian yearning for eternal life." p. 188, The Ratzinger Report

"What is theologically unacceptable here, and socially dangerous, is this mixture of Bible, Christology, politics, sociology and economics. Holy Scripture and theology cannot be misused to absolutize and sacralize a theory concerning the socio-political order. Of its very nature, that order is always contingent. By sacralizing the revolution — mixing up God, Christ and ideologies — they only succeed in producing a dreamy fanaticism that can lead to even worse injustices and oppression, ruining in the praxis what the theory had proposed." p. 190, The Ratzinger Report

"It is also painful to be confronted with the illusion, so essentially un-Christian, which is present among priests and theologians, that a new man and a new world can be created, not by calling each individual to conversion, but only by changing the social and economic structures. For it is precisely personal sin that is in reality at the root of unjust social structures. Those who really desire a more human society need to begin with the root, not with the trunk and branches, of the tree of injustice. The issue here is one of fundamental Christian truths, yet they are deprecatingly dismissed as 'alienating' and 'spiritualistic.'" p. 190, The Ratzinger Report

The word 'painful,' which (then) Cardinal Ratzinger used, makes a striking impact, as this entire process of reading and analyzing Laudato Si' has been quite painful and deeply sad, but necessary. Re-reading Chapter 12 of The Ratzinger Report, on Liberation Theology, enables cutting through much that seems confusing and unexplainable in Laudato Si', and it is highly recommended that the reader consult that Chapter 12 directly. That text was given to the interviewer, Vittorio Messori, prior to the release of Cardinal Ratzinger's Instruction on Certain Aspects of the "Theology of Liberation" on August 6, 1984, with the approval of Pope Saint John Paul II.

Ignatius Press has printed the entire content of the published "Preliminary Notes" to that Instruction as the text of a 'private theologian.' With that understanding, it is possible to address certain excerpts of Laudato Si' which raise questions of collectivism and/or Liberation Theology.

Key questions:

Among the key questions related to this Chapter X are:

1) Can consensus among yet unidentified participants, of unknown skills and motives, ever trump sovereign countries' rights (except perhaps against enemies, or between allies, as in a global war) and still be in accord with the Catechism of the Catholic Church regarding subsidiarity?

2) Why is there any hope that artificial structures like summits, paper agreements or special appointees would be more successful in implementation than was the League of Nations or has been the United Nations?

3) How far has suppression of subsidiarity and/or sabotage of sovereign rights already gone, unbeknownst to citizens of countries most likely to be impacted negatively?

4) When one considers all the reasons the world has not been able to come together for an alleged common good, how would there be anything different in new structures, when weak humans are still weak humans?

5) How is 'common good' to be assessed, and by whom, in a world becoming increasingly degenerate, fragmented, and failing to have made any impact on so many more apparent social evils?

6) What unspoken dangers lurk in the persistent pursuit of even the best of lofty global ambitions, nurturing the erroneous philosophy that the end justifies the means?

7) Who is to determine what is justice and what is merely human covetousness? A functionary? A recipient? A giver?

The inability to satisfactorily answer all these related questions does not prevent such questions from being pondered. Nor does it answer why Bishops' Conferences are so willing to propose strategies on matters for which most of their members have little education and training. Or why those who seek personal power act as if it can be achieved on paper. Jesus taught the whole point of power is that the most powerful is the servant of all, not lording it over them, dispensing penalties and chastisements. ***"… let the greatest among you become as the youngest, and the leader as one who serves."*** (Luke 22:26).

<u>As at the beginning, so also at the end?</u>

On a more biblical level, one might contemplate whether or not there is an effort afoot which grows from the same errors as that infamous project, the Tower of Babel.

In Genesis 11:1-9 we read: ***"Now the whole earth had one language and few words. And as men migrated from the east,*** *they found a plain in the land of Shinar and settled there. And they said to one another, 'Come, let us make bricks, and burn them thoroughly.' And they had brick for stone, and bitumen for mortar. Then they said, 'Come, let us build ourselves a city, and a tower with its top in the heavens, and let us make a name for ourselves, lest we be scattered abroad upon the face of the whole earth.'*

"And the Lord came down to see the city and the tower, which the sons of men had built. And the Lord said, 'Behold, they are one people, and they have all one language; and this is only the beginning of what they will do; and nothing that they propose to do will now be impossible for them. Come, let Us go down, and there confuse their language, that they may not understand one another's speech.'

"So the Lord scattered them abroad from there over the face of all the earth, and they left off building the city. Therefore its name was called Ba'bel, because there the Lord confused the language of all the earth; and from there the Lord scattered them abroad over the face of all the earth."

The Lord did warn that Babel was *"only the beginning."* Relevant quotes from Laudato Si' envision a superstructure of sorts — this time a superstructure of organization, in opposition to subsidiarity, and symbolic of an effort to re-gather the Tower of Babel diaspora from all the earth, to do what belongs to the Second Coming – a re-creation of the physical world.

Does this sound like too much of a stretch? Too untenable? Then consider the grand scale of the pulpit, and these words of Cardinal Ratzinger regarding Liberation Theology: "... fighting for justice and integral liberation, transforming unjust structures into more human ones ... is exercised by repeating in history the gesture by which God raised Jesus, i.e. by giving life to those who are crucified in history. Man has taken over God's gesture — this manifests the whole transformation of the biblical message in an almost tragic way, when one thinks how this attempted imitation of God has worked out in practice and continues to do so." (Page 184, The Ratzinger Report)

Laudato Si' quotations

One should carefully strive to envision what is being created if the philosophy and recommendations of Laudato Si' were to prevail. It is clear that the viewpoint is not that "we are all in this together," but rather that there are strategies to create winners and losers, a pre-judgment disproportionate to work, investment, achievement, need.

"Human beings too are creatures of this world, enjoying a right to life and happiness ... so we cannot fail to consider the effects on people's lives of environmental deterioration ...." (#43)

Further, we should not *"fail to consider the effects on people's lives"* of substituting one injustice for another, or to consider why any potential results from the very perturbation proposed on a world economic system is entirely ignored in the proposals of Laudato Si'.

It is particularly striking how these words of paragraph #43 are blatantly disconnected from what Americans in particular value from the Declaration of Independence, "...life, liberty and the pursuit of happiness." First, it is interesting that 'liberty' has been omitted from this trio. Understandably, that is contradictory to the traditional American value, and to elements of justice as well. Second, experience shows that we don't have a 'right' to happiness, but rather the right to pursue happiness. A guarantee of happiness would only lead to consensus for what constitutes 'happiness' for the majority, without addressing righteousness or individual rights.

This quote in paragraph *#43* is in strange parody to American values, raising questions of 'why' it was written. One conclusion might be that it has a collectivist, socialist viewpoint, with a 'right' to happiness as a demand on the welfare state, but without the expectation of liberty; i.e. just the tyranny of consensus.

As the Declaration of Independence states: "Let Facts be submitted to a candid world." One wonders if, perhaps, the proposal to total all the debts on each ledger (before the Final Judgment, apparently) should go beyond the environment. Will those who have given their lives for the protection of a free world, against tyrants and dictators like Hitler et al, have a credit balance? Will the huge amounts of humanitarian aid rendered after natural disasters be part of the equation? What about major advances in medical breakthroughs? In space exploration? In housing the United Nations? What about the debt the world owes to Israel for having carried forward the line of Christ? What about to martyrs who had no greater love than giving themselves fully? What about the large proportion of worldwide adoptions by Americans? It is dangerous business trying to do a debt census of the world. There is good rationale to let the weeds keep growing with the wheat until Christ returns. Why? Because He said so. (Matthew 13:24-30)

But we set aside for now an 'American viewpoint" and instead examine the gist of the Encyclical's excerpts, which may easily be divided into financial impact, private property, power, and organizational structures. Now we peek at the 'vision' — not with the comments of covetousness made in Chapter VII, but at how many of those same factors offer evidence of collectivism.

Financial Impact

"A true 'ecological debt' exists, particularly between the global north and south, connected to commercial

imbalances with effects on the environment, and the disproportionate use of natural resources by certain countries over long periods of time." (#51) Disproportionate to what? Population? Jobs? Geographical area? Manufacturing resources? Technology produced? Exports? Capital employed?

"The developed countries ought to help pay this debt by significantly limiting their consumption of non-renewable energy and by assisting poorer countries to support policies and programmes of sustainable development." (#52) This repeated theme seems to ignore the benefits of scale, interferes with individual rights, seriously disturbs trade balances and punishes success.

"...the international community has still not reached adequate agreement about the responsibility for paying the costs of ... energy transition." (#165) And it seems that the plan is to impose those opinions against sovereign nations.

"There are too many special interests, and economic interests easily end up trumping the common good ...." (#54) How will the 'common good' be determined? Who is to be the Wizard of Oz behind the curtain? How will conversion of heart ever occur? It cannot be legislated, penalized or bribed.

Private Property

There is also a serious challenge to private property rights in Laudato Si'. Perhaps this section, more than the ambiguity of other sections, clarifies the manipulative social engineering and the questionable motives. One can reasonably ask "Who is the audience being encouraged by these words?"

"In some places, ... the privatization of certain spaces has restricted people's access to places of particular beauty ... 'ecological' neighborhoods ... are closed to outsiders ... we

find beautiful and carefully manicured green spaces in so-called 'safer' areas of cities ...." (#45)

"The principle of the subordination of private property to the universal destination of goods, and thus the right of everyone to their use, is a golden rule of social conduct and 'the first principle of the whole ethical and social order.' The Christian tradition has never recognized the right to private property as absolute or inviolable, and has stressed the social purpose of all forms of private property." (#93) [Context not verified.]

"[Pope] Saint John Paul II ... explained that 'the Church does indeed defend the legitimate right to private property but she also teaches no less clearly that there is always a social mortgage on all private property, in order that goods may serve the general purpose that God gave them.'" (#93) [Context not verified.]

<u>Power</u>

"To ensure economic freedom from which all can effectively benefit, restraints occasionally have to be imposed on those possessing greater resources and financial power." (#129) It is one thing to impose restraints such as requiring clean air or properly treated discharge. It is entirely a different imposition to enforce anti-competitive limits on production, for example, or to undermine world capital structures or the sovereignty of nations.

"...the time has come to accept decreased growth in some parts of the world, in order to provide resources for other places to experience healthy growth." (#193) Again, the basic question looms of 'who' will be given the authority to interpret what is truly just? Where is any basic analysis to demonstrate that suppressing one economy will actually

stimulate another? What test cases, if any, prove meaningful success for 'Liberal-Nation Theology?'

"A global consensus is essential for confronting the deeper problems, which cannot be resolved by unilateral actions on the part of individual countries." (#164) Who empowers global consensus? Who will exercise that power? Who can delegate that power? (See coveting discussion in Chapter VII.)

"...this Encyclical welcomes dialogue with everyone so that together we can seek paths of liberation." (#64) Given concerns about the infiltration of Liberation Theology, the word choice seems odd. Its meaning is unclear but, generally, dialogue with everyone is dialogue with no one.

Organization and Structures

"...we still lack the culture needed to confront this crisis. We lack leadership capable of striking out on new paths and meeting the needs of the present with concern for all and without prejudice towards coming generations." (#53) Crisis? Global leadership by one person or even a committee (pre-Second Coming) is a myth which enslaves, not sets free. Praise be Jesus Christ, the One and Only King.

"...The establishment of a legal framework which can set clear boundaries and ensure the protection of ecosystems has become indispensable, otherwise the new power structures based on the techno-economic paradigm may overwhelm not only our politics but also freedom and justice." (#53) Aren't *"freedom and justice"* already overwhelmed victims of collectivist propaganda? Who or what are these *"new power structures"* and who appoints or elects the members? If incipient, capable leadership could emerge, would it not have already done so?

"We urgently need a humanism capable of bringing together the different fields of knowledge, including economics, in the service of a more integral and integrating vision." (#141) This is reminiscent of the "central planning" of socialist countries.

"...social ecology is necessarily institutional, and gradually extends to the whole of society ...." (#142)

"International negotiations cannot make significant progress due to positions taken by countries which place their national interest above the global common good." (#169) Should not this statement be clarified to say "alleged global common good," since so much is unproven, except the ever-persistent desire for more cash from the wealthier nations? What countries' representatives, assuming the responsibilities for which they were elected, would not see their job as primarily protecting their own nations' interests? How does subsidiarity fit into these concepts, if there is denial of free will of the individual, and denial of sovereign rights of nations?

"Enforceable international agreements are urgently needed, since local authorities are not always capable of effective intervention." (#173) One would trust that incapable local authorities are the business and responsibility of those who elect them and, hopefully, will not be named as 'functionaries' for higher office. "Enforceable" – how? An international police force? There seems to be an undue emphasis on punishment and penalties, rather than on incentives and conversion of heart.

"What is needed ... is an agreement on systems of governance for the whole range of so-called 'global commons.'" (#174) This is a continuation of the myth that if agreements are reached they are therefore implementable.

"It is essential to devise stronger and more efficiently organized international institutions, with functionaries who are appointed fairly by agreement among national governments, and empowered to impose sanctions." (#175) And in this very sentence, discussed in Chapter IX relative to an out-of-context quote attributed to Pope Benedict, all the dangerous elements are exposed in a clear statement of how someone might try to argue that the 'end justifies the means.'

From whence comes the hope that nations, governments and politicians, so roundly criticized for inability (or unwillingness) to act, to rule, to govern and sanction will then appoint (unelected) 'functionaries' in a super secular and greedy world who will be effective, responsible and above reproach? Doesn't the entire argument collapse on itself? Or else, perhaps confessionals will no longer be needed, and people will be able to transcend all temptation and greed and intimidation? More likely, the faults of a persistently fallen human race will not be erased by new ways to manipulate, but rather be stimulated by the opportunity.

What about the poor?

"The same mindset which stands in the way of making radical decisions to reverse the trend of global warming also stands in the way of the goal of eliminating poverty. A more responsible overall approach is needed to deal with both problems: the reduction of pollution and the development of poorer countries and regions." (#175) The logic chain is again missing between the two assertions.

Without denying the need of each soul to reach out in charity, nevertheless we cannot deny the truth of Christ's words in Mark 14:7: ***"For you always have the poor with you, and whenever you will, you can do good to them; but you will***

not always have Me." The *"goal of eliminating poverty"* is not a realistic goal; 'global warming' is a lame stalking horse.

Marxism, collectivism, socialism?

If some of the above statements in the Encyclical sound suspiciously like socialism or marxism or collectivism (i.e. the practice or principle of giving a group priority over each individual in it; the theory and practice of the ownership of land and the means of production by the people or by the state), it would not be surprising. Perennial error again swings the pendulum to the left.

Certainly, this is NOT to say that Pope Francis is or is not a marxist, as not enough information is provided. Rather, it is to note the risks of associating the Catholic Church with those who are socialists, who will misuse and abuse all that many hold dear, being especially divisive within the Church, e.g. against those whose God-given Freedoms are enshrined in their culture, and bred in their bones.

Messori recounts Cardinal Ratzinger's words:

"...in the West, the marxist myth has lost its attraction for the young and even for the workers. There is an attempt, therefore, to export it to the Third World on the part of those intellectuals who actually live outside countries dominated by 'real Socialism', indeed, it is only where marxism-leninism [sic] is *not* in control that there are still people who take its illusory 'scientific truths' seriously." (Page 187, The Ratzinger Report)

"[Cardinal Ratzinger]...went on to tell me how dismayed he was by reading many of these theologians. A continual refrain is this: 'Man must be liberated from the chains of politico-economic oppression; the reforms are not enough to liberate him, indeed they lead away from liberation; what is necessary is revolution, and the only way to bring about a revolution is to summon people to the class struggle.' [Will history interpret

Laudato Si' as a summons to a class struggle?] Yet those who repeat all this seem to have no concrete and practical idea how a society could be organized after the revolution. They limit themselves to repeating that the revolution must be brought about." (Page 189, The Ratzinger Report)

It is difficult to conclude that such 'revolution' *isn't* part of the underpinning of Laudato Si', or that class warfare *isn't* stimulated by putting targets on the backs of those blessed with more than others. If it were only a matter of evangelizing the individual soul, it would be understandable. But to pit souls against each other in what can become a free-for-all power grab is divisive to the Body of Christ.

The implied socialism of Laudato Si' is consistent with the historic context of its one-dimensionality. The discord is not because one group has more universities than another, or because one group has more healthy people than another, or one group has deeper faith than another, or any of myriad comparisons. It is about money, which, in itself, is highly 'over-valued.' For value, money requires something to be done with it. The plan does not go deep enough to answer the question: "For what use?" It seems more about 'taking away' than using the money for productive policy. But perhaps there is more in the unrevealed plans. We just aren't told.

The Practical Contrast

Opening Church doors to offer needed charity and care during times of crisis is a valid appeal to souls, and so very different from rioters' looting local stores of merchandise and burning them down during civil unrest. Free will vs. violence is one distinction, for example. Again, it seems, the collectivist mindset has difficulty distinguishing between means and end. Rather, it appears to seek the 'leadership' position to dictate which shelves to empty first, and the right to direct the mob.

Luke 12:13-15 reads: ***"One of the multitude said to Him, 'Teacher, bid my brother divide the inheritance with me.' But He said to him, 'Man, who made Me a judge or divider over you?' And He said to them, 'Take heed, and beware of all covetousness; for a man's life does not consist in the abundance of his possessions.'"***

If Christ refused to be a divider of goods, if He saw covetousness in focusing on goods, by what arrogance would an international body be constructed to do what Christ refused to do? And by what naïveté would Catholics want to participate?

Chapter XI

<u>"Who Am I to Judge?"</u>

Pope Francis made world headlines in his press interview aloft, flying back from World Youth Day in Rio de Janiero in 2013, when asked about the status of a reputedly 'gay' priest. His reply "Who am I to judge?" became a rallying cry for LGBT life style to be legitimized by the Catholic Church (which clearly is impossible to happen, and have it still be the Catholic Church, founded by Jesus Christ.)

Faithful Catholics, knowledgeable regarding Church teaching, trustingly strained to understand the words to mean "If a person repents of his sins and is forgiven by God, who am I to decide otherwise?" Prelates of good will tried to do the same; some were demeaned and some apparently ousted as a result.

Unfortunately, the popular media and the subsequent lack of papal explanation simply allowed a runaway wish list of aspirations, each more liberal than the preceding, each speculating that perhaps the Catholic Church was going to finally 'permit sin.' The Synod, held in October 2014, only made matters worse due to its foggy language, leaked documents, poor and unmatched translations and questionable motivations, sowing doubt where previously there had been clarity. And, if not for the first time, at least for perhaps the most significant time since the Arian Heresy, Catholics knew that a significant percentage of their prelates do not believe what the Church teaches. May all souls be protected from those prelates. It is unfortunate that heretics aren't required to wear bells, like the lepers of old. But at least Pope Francis knows who the heretics are, so he can meet his responsibility to protect us against them. St. Nicholas, pray for us!

It is worth mentioning the recent track record of poor Vatican communications, as a prelude to sorting out some seemingly quite harsh language in Laudato Si', which threatens to cause further division within the Church. In the Encyclical, there is a lack of clarification, and a sense of 'you know to whom I'm referring,' without being specific. And, very unlike our expectation of teaching documents, there is an ambiguity which does a disservice to Truth, and to souls.

Is Laudato Si' a 'judgmental' document?

In this Chapter, some Laudato Si' statements are listed, without explaining what may well be unexplainable, but which language yields a fruit that spotlights the risk of division, consternation, defensiveness, confusion, pain and alienation. Not only the content, but also the tone, contributes to such impact.

These comments are not a judgment of Pope Francis, since we don't know his motives, or even the accuracy of his translators. The quotes are put forward hoping to invoke that same spirit of "Who am I to judge?" regarding what we understand Pope Francis to have written. The reader may consider whether or not any of these quotes is judgmental or accusatory or sarcastic, or how the points might have been better phrased in the spirit of unity, charity and compassion.

So, we quote directly, letting the reader form conclusions about the objectives of each statement. There are many quotes which might have been used, but the limited ones selected are those which seem to ascribe a questionable motive to others, to people, groups or nations, notwithstanding the occasional use of the first person plural pronouns 'we,' 'our' and 'us.'

Affluent individuals, multinational companies and northern hemisphere countries, in particular, seem to be targeted.

Perhaps, surprisingly, the Church and other organized religions seem to escape all criticism; this will be addressed in Chapter XIV.

Regrettably, there are few proposals for remedy other than loss of subsidiarity to a theoretical collectivist power, as described in prior chapters, e.g. through allocation of financial penalties by 'functionaries' against sovereign governments. It is not the purpose to debate again what was previously covered, but only to convey what some may see as an attitude of accusation in Laudato Si'. It is only fair to point out that there may simply be a misunderstanding. Since Christ Himself did not come to condemn, one must be careful in attributing condemnation to others. Nevertheless, these direct quotes from Laudato Si', with its frequently seeking 'money' settlements, raises questions of motivation. So, too, does the harsh and unmitigated tone of some allegations.

Excerpts (and accusations?) from Laudato Si'

"...many efforts to seek concrete solutions to the environmental crisis have proved ineffective, not only because of powerful opposition but also because of a more general lack of interest. Obstructionist attitudes, even on the part of believers, can range from denial of the problem to indifference, nonchalant resignation or blind confidence in technical solutions." (#14)

"Many of those who possess more resources and economic or political power seem mostly to be concerned with masking the problems or concealing their symptoms, simply making efforts to reduce some of the negative impacts of climate change." (#26)

"Our world has a grave social debt towards the poor who lack access to drinking water, because they are denied

the right to a life consistent with their inalienable dignity. This debt can be paid partly by an increase in funding ...." (#30)

"We seem to think that we can substitute an irreplaceable and irretrievable beauty with something which we have created ourselves." (#34)

"Caring for ecosystems demands far-sightedness, since no one looking for quick and easy profit is truly interested in their preservation .... We can be silent witnesses to terrible injustices if we think that we can obtain significant benefits ...." (#36)

"...there are 'proposals to internationalize the Amazon which only serve the economic interests of transnational corporations.'" (#38)

"...many professionals, opinion makers, communications media and centres of power, being located in affluent urban areas, are far removed from the poor, with little direct contact with their problems. They live and reason from the comfortable position of a high level of development and a quality of life well beyond the reach of the majority of the world's population .... This lack ... can lead to a numbing of conscience and to tendentious analyses which neglect parts of reality ...." (#49)

"...a minority believes that it has the right to consume in a way which can never be universalized ...." (#50)

"There is also ... pollution produced by companies which operate in less developed countries in ways they could never do at home, in the countries in which they raise their capital: ... 'often the businesses which operate this way are multinationals.'" (#51)

"The warming caused by huge consumption on the part of some rich countries has repercussions on the poorest areas of the world, especially Africa, where a rise in temperature, together with drought, has proved devastating for farming …." (#51) Note: like many other unsupported statements in Laudato Si', again there is no footnote citation as a data source.

"The foreign debt of poor countries has become a way of controlling them …. [D]eveloping countries … continue to fuel the development of richer countries at the cost of their own present and future … [ownership] is structurally perverse … [D]eveloped countries ought to help pay this debt by significantly limiting their consumption of non-renewable energy …. [G]lobalization of indifference …." (#52) Is it really a 'zero-sum game'?

"There are too many special interests, and economic interests easily end up trumping the common good and manipulating information so that their own plans will not be affected." (#54) Few of the generalizations are backed up with specific examples or footnotes.

"The alliance between the economy and technology ends up sidelining anything unrelated to its immediate interests … the most one can expect is superficial rhetoric, sporadic acts of philanthropy and perfunctory expressions of concern for the environment, whereas any genuine attempt by groups within society to introduce change is viewed as a nuisance based on romantic illusions or an obstacle to be circumvented." (#54)

"People may well have a growing ecological sensitivity but it has not succeeded in changing their harmful habits of consumption which, rather than decreasing, appear to

be growing all the more. A simple example is the increasing use and power of air-conditioning." (#55)

"...human beings contrive to feed their self-destructive vices: trying not to see them, trying not to acknowledge them, delaying the important decisions and pretending that nothing will happen." (#59)

"...'twenty percent of the world's population consumes resources at a rate that robs the poor nations and future generations of what they need to survive.'" (#95) Again, no reference to the source of these data is given.

"Some circles [show] ... no interest in more balanced levels of production, a better distribution of wealth, concern for the environment and the rights of future generations. Their behavior shows that for them maximizing profits is enough." (#109)

"...'the technological mind sees nature as an insensate order, as a cold body of facts, as a mere 'given,' as an object of utility, as raw material to be hammered into useful shape; it views the cosmos similarly as a mere 'space' into which objects can be thrown with complete indifference.'" (#115) In my personal experience I have often found scientists to be even more fascinated with the physical world and its wonder than many with no technological training, who seem to take it for granted.

"...we should not be surprised to find, in conjunction with the omnipresent technocratic paradigm and the cult of unlimited human power, the rise of a relativism which sees everything as irrelevant unless it serves one's own immediate interests." (#122)

"The culture of relativism is the same disorder which drives one person to take advantage of another, to treat others as mere objects, imposing forced labor on them or enslaving them to pay their debts. The same kind of thinking leads to the sexual exploitation of children and abandonment of the elderly ... human trafficking, organized crime, the drug trade, commerce in blood diamonds and the fur of endangered species ... buying the organs of the poor for resale.... This same 'use and throw away' logic generates so much waste, because of the disordered desire to consume more than what is really necessary." (#123) By such logic, every overweight person, consuming 'more than what is really necessary,' would be implicated to some degree in heinous crimes. Obviously the problems are far more complex, as is human nature. Simplistic accusations illustrate the risk of thinking any particular organization can ever bridle the concupiscence of a fallen nature, especially large collectivist organizations with their ultimate unaccountability resulting in being responsible to no one, because they can hide behind being responsible to everyone.

Should not the emphasis, rather, be toward conversion of souls than toward super-sizing organizational structure and its impositions? Railing against multinationals hardly seems to create argument for still larger enforcers, whose individual members are as corruptible as anyone else.

"An interdependent world not only makes us more conscious of the negative effects of certain lifestyles and models of production and consumption which affect us all; more importantly, it motivates us to ensure that solutions are proposed from a global perspective, and not simply to defend the interests of a few countries." (#164)

"Reducing greenhouse gases requires honesty, courage and responsibility, above all on the part of those countries which are more powerful and pollute the most." (#169) One point on which the Encyclical is relatively silent is that the burden, if it were to be assigned, would more properly apply not only to countries that pollute, but also to the recipients of the benefits of the polluting manufacturing or technology made available to them as customers, and those for whom jobs are created. Probably few countries would willingly give up products and technologies they want or need in order to minimize the associated pollution. Also, for that reason, one wonders about the high level of prioritization skewed to environmental matters, relative to other subjects to which papal encyclicals might be addressed.

"Political activity on the local level could also be directed to modifying consumption." (#180) Rationing almost always has, as its result, creation of a black market, and black markets suffer the side effects of crime, and further manipulation by those with substantial financial ability or oversight. Another ugly side of *"modifying consumption"* comes from the 'sustainability advocates,' who favor fewer people alive and consuming. The Encyclical skirts the issue, supporting the sustainability objective but being silent on its strategy.

"While some are concerned only with financial gain, and others with holding on to or increasing their power, what we are left with are conflicts or spurious agreements where the last thing either party is concerned about is caring for the environment and protecting those who are most vulnerable." (#198)

"Obsession with a consumerist lifestyle, above all when few people are capable of maintaining it, can only lead to violence and mutual destruction." (#204) This is not an untypical summons to class warfare.

"...we are unconcerned about caring for things for the sake of others; we fail to set limits on ourselves in order to avoid the suffering of others or the deterioration of our surroundings." (#208)

In a general sense, we can see that much of the theme in these words, directed against others (people, companies, nations), is about transfer of power, from those who have it (and at least, to some extent, have earned it, inherited it or invested in it) to those with more limited power, even within their own borders, where, for a variety of reasons, legitimate power with a servant mindset has apparently not been fully or faithfully exercised.

As one reviews the excerpts above, perhaps it would have been better for Pope Francis to have used his question "Who am I to judge?" from his travels aloft, one more time, regarding those portrayed as enemies of the environment or of ecology. When mentioned earlier that there is a certain sadness or darkness in Laudato Si', this section in particular seems to be related, and it feels more alienating than uniting. I do wish that Laudato Si' at least had emulated the gentleness of Pope Benedict's writings.

Finally, without knowing reasons or purpose, motivation or intent, we can simply recall and pray the words of Sacred Scripture:

"Fathers, do not provoke your children to anger, but bring them up in the discipline and instruction of the Lord." (Ephesians 6:4)

"Fathers, do not provoke your children, lest they become discouraged." (Colossians 3:21)

Chapter XII
Infallibility?

Obviously, the answer to the question of whether or not Laudato Si' is infallible cannot be given fully in this space. An opinion can of course be offered, but it is without authority. Nevertheless, questions can be raised for discussion in the consideration of what individual obligations Catholics might have (or not have) to follow on any particular course or instruction in Laudato Si'. In that spirit, the following seven points are noted:

1. Lack of a Claim of Infallibility

Upon completing the reading of Laudato Si', one notices the 'prominent absence' of any words claiming 'infallibility.' For example, in the words of Pope Saint John Paul II, regarding the impossibility of women's ordination, he declared clearly and significantly in Ordinatio Sacerdotalis (Ref. E-11):

"Wherefore, in order that all doubt may be removed regarding a matter of great importance, a matter which pertains to the Church's divine constitution itself, in virtue of my ministry of confirming the brethren (cf. Lk 22:32) I declare that the Church has no authority whatsoever to confer priestly ordination on women and that this judgment is to be definitively held by all the Church's faithful.

Invoking an abundance of divine assistance upon you, venerable brothers, and upon all the faithful, I impart my apostolic blessing.

From the Vatican, on May 22, the Solemnity of Pentecost, in the year 1994, the sixteenth of my Pontificate."

Even such clear words have sometimes been parsed beyond recognition, and murmured against by those who are adamant about coveting women's ordination. They balk at the lack of the specific word "infallible." Nevertheless, the intent of Pope Saint John Paul II does seem quite clear, and was also subsequently upheld by Pope Benedict XVI.

The words of Pope Francis in Laudato Si' contain no such claim of infallibility, but actually contain words and implications which would likely weaken any claim to infallibility. That is not to say that a papal writing doesn't deserve, on its own merit and out of respect, some attention to the message. That is precisely what has driven this particular examination of Laudato Si' in this present writing. And it is the reason we examine two sentences which might be the strongest claims for infallibility, yet seem quite weak.

2. Consideration of two sentences which might be used to imply infallibility

Only two sentences were found in the entire Encyclical which hint at infallibility; however, hinting is hardly strong enough to be an effective proclamation of infallibility. Here are the two specific, somewhat personally oriented, papal sentences:

a. *"I* [i.e. Pope Francis] *will offer some inspired guidelines for human development to be found in the treasure of Christian spiritual experience."* *(#15)* One might wonder if the use of the word *'inspired'* is claiming that this Encyclical is Divine Private Revelation, but even that would seem to be only a very tenuous connection to claiming infallibility. Private revelation is not equivalent to an infallible declaration. Papal responsibility must protect the Deposit of Faith already received, even as understanding of divine revelation matures. For what argument or example can be set forth of any doctrinal revelation after the death of the last Apostle, binding on the Deposit of Faith? Or that any novel, revelatory declaration has actually been claimed or attempted by the Catholic Church?

If Pope Francis' word *"inspired"* were intended to imply infallibility, it would likely have been much more specific. Thus, the word *"inspired"* makes more sense as personal insight, rather than as Divine Revelation. This is especially so without consistent repetition or clarification of an intended claim, and without first developing the specific areas to which a claim of any divinely inspired revelation might arguably try to be applied. Moreover, given their placement quite early in the Encyclical, such words are difficult to attribute to anything specifically covered by a claim of private revelation.

b. *"It is my* [Pope Francis'] *hope that this Encyclical Letter, which is now added to the body of the Church's social teaching, can help us to acknowledge the appeal, immensity and urgency of the challenge we face."* (#15) The proximity of this text to the one mentioned above would seem to put it in the same class as a general or orienting statement, not as a specific claim of infallibility.

Moreover, adding the Encyclical to the *"body of the Church's social teaching"* specifically reminds us that much of the Church's *"social teaching"* has not been claimed to be infallible, and some may not even be specifically in the area of 'faith and morals' (which is the domain to which claims of infallibility are restricted). Therefore, any claim of infallibility based on the *"body of ... social teaching"* also seems weak. Whatever Pope Francis' intent is with the wording of these two specific statements in paragraph #15, it seems well-removed from an infallibility claim.

One argument not made, but one fears might be made in the future, is that "everything" is in the moral category (unless it is faith). But such a definition of "moral" would remove the need to have defined any limitations on the scope of infallibility, as there then would be none. So, such a theoretical argument for infallibility fails in logic and history.

3. The Encyclical is broadly addressed to the entire world without specific binding language or claim

The address to the entire world raises two questions: 1) Is the Pope's addressing the entire world and asking for its input a de facto invitation to non-Christians to shape the teaching of the Church? If so, how would that orient the current content of the Encyclical toward even an illusion of infallibility? 2) Doesn't such a worldwide invitation for input at least partially impair any consideration of infallibility for Laudato Si' by positioning it as an incomplete work?

Relevant quotes include:

"...faced as we are with global environmental deterioration, I wish to address every person living on the planet." (#3)

"...I would like to enter into dialogue with all people about our common home." (#3)

"We need a conversation which includes everyone." (#14)

4. The Encyclical's strong call for debate and discussion implies a meaningful possibility of change

The very implication of changing what has been already been written, based on worldwide discussion or on any other input to dialogue (including possible refutation of 'global warming' and 'climate change' premises, or including clarification of certain currently ambiguous statements), could apparently negate any concern that the Encyclical, as it is now written, binds infallibly. There are many Encyclical entries inviting debate and dialogue. Here are a few:

"...the need for forthright and honest debate ...." (#16)

"Today, however, we have to realize that a true ecological approach always becomes a social approach; it must integrate questions of justice in debates on the environment, so as to hear both the cry of the earth and the cry of the poor." (#49)

"On many concrete questions, the Church has no reason to offer a definitive opinion; she knows that honest debate must be encouraged among experts, while respecting divergent views." (#61)

"A broad, responsible scientific and social debate needs to take place, one capable of considering all the available information and of calling things by their name." (#135)

"This necessarily entails reflection and debate about the conditions required for the life and survival of society, and the honesty needed to question certain models of development, production and consumption." (#138)

"Even as this Encyclical was being prepared, the debate was intensifying." (#169)

"We need to stop thinking in terms of 'interventions' to save the environment in favour of policies developed and debated by all interested parties." (#183)

"But I am concerned to encourage an honest and open debate so that particular interests or ideologies will not prejudice the common good." (#188)

5. A strong call for discussion by every individual is without a practical mechanism for implementation

The call for discussion is broad-based. Some discussion may be narrower on individual projects, but much seems to be directed to a worldwide exchange which has no mechanism to effect even the dialogue, let alone any implementation. In simpler terms, it would seem that God doesn't ask of us what it is not possible to do. Thus, the impracticality of worldwide discussions (with or without the "one world" approach) in itself weakens any claim to infallibility. It may even, under test, become the stumbling block to the very implementations which Pope Francis seeks.

Moreover, with even the Synod of 2014 unable to issue an English translation consistent with the Italian, for example, what hope can there be of avoiding manipulation of the dialogue? Or of defying the re-creation of the Tower of Babel?

"We need a conversation which includes everyone, since the environmental challenge we are undergoing, and its human roots, concern and affect us all." (#14)

"Discussions are needed in which all those directly or indirectly affected (farmers, consumers, civil authorities, scientists, seed producers, people living near fumigated fields, and others) can make known their problems and concerns, and have access to adequate and reliable information in order to make decisions for the common good, present and future." (#135)

"Honesty and truth are needed in scientific and political discussions; these should not be limited to the issue of whether or not a particular project is permitted by law." (#183)

"If politics shows itself incapable of breaking such a perverse logic, and remains caught up in inconsequential discussions, we will continue to avoid facing the major problems of humanity." (#197) The major problem of humanity is sin, which flows from concupiscence, from not

giving God His due. Compared to that reality, environmental claims seem much less urgent.

6. Non-specificity of action items

Laudato Si' does not read as having a narrow drawing of potentially infallible issues, but rather more like an op-ed than a Church Teaching, like a laundry list of environmental wishes.

Even if Laudato Si' were destined, at some point, to be binding infallibly in certain subject areas, the action items are weak, scattered and without clarity as to exactly what is being asked, and in what priority order. (See Chapter XIII.)

The Encyclical, taken as a whole, is disturbing; unfortunately, it reads more like a rant against the world environmental and ecological situation than prescriptive for spiritual growth or required obedience, with very little expectation of individual readers' 'doing' anything much different from the daily lives they already lead. That is understandable, since much of what is decried and much of what is desired is out of the hands and influence of individuals. However, there are a few specific actions suggested, relatively minor, and those will be covered in the next chapter, for the sake of completeness.

7. An ironic reflection

It would be difficult to close this Chapter XII on Infallibility without reflecting on an ironic context to Vatican I, the first Council since Trent, three centuries earlier. Pope Pius IX summoned the Council in 1869, targeting 'modern errors.' Vatican I was deemed to be a pastoral council, reinforcing or restating what was already Church dogma. Papal infallibility had long been understood and accepted in the Church; e.g. when Peter, the first Pope, made the decision not to require circumcision of the Gentiles.

In the recent book "History of the Catholic Church," by respected historian Dr. James Hitchcock (Ref. E-12), a brief history is recounted of Vatican I, and the details of its members wrestling with a statement on Papal Infallibility. Hitchcock writes (page 366): "The idea of papal infallibility was already widely accepted, and Pius did not ask the Council to approve it, lest it appear that he received his authority from the Council. He merely waited until the Council voted to proclaim it" but he exerted some "... strong pressure on wavering bishops."

Hitchcock notes that "Some bishops were troubled by the doctrine of infallibility because they thought it implied that they received their authority solely from the pope, rather than being direct successors of the Apostles." ... "A preliminary vote showed 451 in favor of the dogma, 62 in favor "conditionally", and 88 opposed. On the eve of its solemn ratification, the opposition leaders agreed that, rather than vote ... 'it does not please me', they would absent themselves."

Apparently all but two of those in opposition left the Council. However, Napoleon III's troops were protecting Rome from the Italian armies, so there may well have been other reasons for hasty departures. A schism occurred in Germany, in particular, thereafter, with the "Old Catholic" breakaway. Vatican I was not officially "closed" until Vatican II.

Hitchcock summarizes: "Infallibility was understood as encompassing only matters of faith and morals that were solemnly proclaimed by the pope ex cathedra ... a limitation necessary in order to exclude the doctrinal errors of some popes .... The pope could not create new dogmas but merely authoritatively define what were already the Church's beliefs."

Herein lies the irony. Some bishops of Vatican I objected to a clear, bold statement on papal infallibility because, in part, it appeared to extend the Pope's power, although infallibility was already well accepted. But the Holy Spirit works in mysterious ways. Now, about 146 years later, we can understand that the clarifications of Vatican I, rather than intrusively limiting the bishops' power, merely placed constraints and limitations on the infallibility claim of any pope, especially through the restriction to "matters of faith and morals." That reality may well be a source of comfort to bishops concerned with directions Synods may take, and priorities of various encyclicals.

Perhaps, under the Holy Spirit's guidance and protection, that which once seemed to be strengthening papal power has in reality clarified for the Faithful their right to cling to and protect their faith, and not to be seduced into enjoying the 'flavor of the month' so easily chosen by sects and faith traditions which rely on their own elders' opinions and political pressures, rather than doctrinal infallibility. Indeed, the Holy Spirit works mysteriously, preparing so many years in advance.

Come Holy Spirit and abide with us!

Chapter XIII
<u>Individual Action Plan</u>

Most of the prior chapters in this monograph have dealt with the general principles which Pope Francis promulgated through the Church's Teaching Office and, in a number of cases, with his personal opinions. It is difficult to consistently distinguish teaching from opinion but, since Laudato Si' appears, at least on its surface, not to be binding, the need to distinguish minutely is abated. Nevertheless, respect for any pope's writing is sufficient reason to search for statements in Laudato Si' which suggest individual actions, in contrast to the more obvious macro recommendations for various governmental or other organizational initiatives.

The question, were I sitting in the room with Pope Francis, would be "Your Holiness, what would you have *me* do?"

<u>Examples of matters not included: water and food</u>

To isolate the specific individual actions, it is also necessary to leave out all the generalizations, all the calls for actions other than from individuals, and then attempt to answer the question from the pew: "But what can 'I' do about environmental and ecological issues which would matter to God?"

The following discussion will leave out implied calls for action which identify needs but not how to solve those needs, such as certain remarks regarding water and food, for example. Nevertheless, let us not forget that giving drink to the thirsty and food to the hungry are already two necessary Corporal Works of Mercy.

<u>Water</u>: Pope Francis particularly decries the waste of water. For those living in areas with abundant water, providing care

to lawns, golf courses and gardens, washing cars, taking daily showers, even visiting waterparks, how are individual conservationists of good heart to 'save' water for people living in remote desert areas? Water cannot be shipped long distances cost effectively, and self-denial may have some spiritual benefit but, for others, it may be a health risk. Since there is no specific action called for on this matter in Laudato Si', it therefore is not included in this particular discussion below. However, please see Appendix B for an example of how one New York State parish, in an area of abundant water, provided for an arid village in Kenya.

Food: Another example would be Pope Francis' comment against wasting food, which applies to many communities and families considered affluent on a worldwide basis. Laudato Si' states:

"…'whenever food is thrown out it is as if it were stolen from the table of the poor.'" (#50)

Such a dramatic statement has an element of both truth and drama to it, but how is an individual to respond beyond some of the methods like food kitchens and pantries, often run by church communities? In the United States there are restrictions and government regulations on recycling food, such as from restaurants, and especially related to USDA and FDA guidelines, including labeling.

Pricing structure in most stores prevents one from buying only what is needed, say, a half head of lettuce, or 3 eggs, or a third of a loaf of bread. And, living at some distance in more rural communities, we can see it may be better to buy something in the market which may not be fully used, rather than driving again, many miles roundtrip, if and when it may actually be needed, thus wasting time and fuel.

It is already reported that over half the U.S. population uses food stamps, paid by taxes from the other half. One might argue for more subsidy, as a work of charity, but is it charity if it endorses and supports a decadent or slothful lifestyle? Or if we differentially fund the more 'affluent poor' in the United States at the expense of many others in the world who have much greater need?

In St. Paul's second letter to the Thessalonians he writes: ***"For even when we were with you, we gave you this command: If any one will not work, let him not eat. For we hear that some of you are living in idleness, mere busybodies, not doing any work. Now such persons we command and exhort in the Lord Jesus Christ to do their work in quietness and to earn their own living."*** (2 Thessalonians 3:10-12)

Unfortunately, some of the ill-thought-out assistance which causes the recipient to lose human dignity by having no expectations of contribution to the community may be wreaking havoc on souls on both sides of the equation. The question is not one of feel-good individual actions to advance a pet agenda, but rather it should be all about the good of souls.

<u>What individual actions are suggested?</u>

Statements of genuine concern, not translated to specific individual actions in Laudato Si', are not included below, because it is not the function of this review and dialogue on Laudato Si' to try to extend the general words of the Encyclical to specific actions. That is a role for implementation groups. This chapter only lists those specific, identifiable actions in the Encyclical for which individual actions are suggested.

1.　<u>Dialogue and discussion</u> regarding the environmental and ecological issues raised are mentioned prominently throughout the Encyclical. Not only does such dialogue refer to the

Encyclical itself, but also to dialogue between individuals who are affected. Such dialogue would seem to be appropriate, both as a means of educating and involving people to take care of their communities, and to mobilize broader, well-aligned efforts. However, most Catholics are unlikely to read the full Encyclical. If their input is really being expected, it will require action by parishes and dioceses to make it happen.

2.	Involvement: Laudato Si' states: *"...local individuals and groups can make a real difference. They are able to instill a greater sense of responsibility, a strong sense of community, a readiness to protect others, a spirit of creativity and a deep love for the land. They are also concerned about what they will eventually leave to their children and grandchildren." (#179)*

A good local example might be how individuals in some areas were able to unite in various ways regarding hydrofracking concerns. Spontaneous action from citizens can have impact when it flows from rational dialogue. It becomes complicated by government interference, when the focus is to confront the government, coerce the taxpayer, or repay political obligations rather than seeking better ways to care for the people and for the environment.

Unfortunately, the Encyclical itself has an apparent clash between the principle of subsidiarity (see Chapter IX), with actions rising from the bottom up, in which needs and possibilities are generated and implemented by those closest to the problem, and an imposition of top down rules and penalties on a worldwide scale, in a collectivist setting. The two methods inevitably clash at the point where strategies conflict, and then power flexes its muscle.

3.	Prayer: Laudato Si' issues the following call for prayer:

"We believers cannot fail to ask God for a positive outcome to the present discussions, so that future generations will not have to suffer the effects of our ill-advised delays." (#169)

Or shall we simply pray that all the resources of humanity, limited as they are, be directed toward what God considers most important? May we not also pray for preservation of subsidiarity? And respect for the free will of all individuals? It seems rather doubtful that the people of a free nation would ask for a collectivist solution. Yet Laudato Si' ignores how such serious issues can be approached, yet still respect the rights of sovereign nations and of human dignity.

Specific comments on the prayers offered near the end of Laudato Si' will be discussed in Chapter XV. Certainly we recognize that prayer is needed both for individuals and for communities and, in that sense, we all have a call to participate, petitioning that God's Will may be done, rather than the will of human organizations using short-sighted solutions. Much discernment is needed to determine where, indeed, is God moving in this situation? Just possibly, reinstitution of the Tower of Babel may not be the plan.

4.   <u>Specific Actions</u> are recommended in Chapter Five of Laudato Si': *"Lines of Approach and Action."* The following excerpts show some of Pope Francis' focus:

"...[using] less heating and [wearing] warmer clothes ... avoiding the use of plastic and paper, reducing water consumption, separating refuse, cooking only what can reasonably be consumed, showing care for other living beings, using public transport or car-pooling, planting trees, turning off unnecessary lights.... Reusing something instead of immediately discarding it...." (#211)

"Ecological education ..." (#213) See Chapter XVI, Section J.

"...personal qualities of self-control and willingness to learn from one another." (#214)

"...stop and give thanks to God before and after meals." (#227)

There is a tension between addressing every person, inviting individual dialogue, yet recognizing the limited ability of individual persons to achieve macro change. Laudato Si' states:

"Isolated individuals can lose their ability and freedom to escape the utilitarian mindset, and end up prey to an unethical consumerism bereft of social or ecological awareness. Social problems must be addressed by community networks and not simply by the sum of individual good deeds." (#219) Yet, doesn't everything first have to start with, and then depend upon, individuals' cooperating with God's graces? And how is this excerpt #219 to be reconciled with the call for specific individual actions in paragraph #211? And the praise for individual actions in #179?

Such limitations raise the question not only of tension between individuals and collectivist power, but also within individuals' own limited resources and their personal obligations. Just how important is proposed change involving the environment in contrast to other activities to which we are called in spiritual and moral obligation?

The only truly unsustainable, nonrenewable resource is our own time

Therefore, to be principally consumed with environmental and ecological matters detracts, in the sense of time and energy, from even higher spiritual activities, i.e. worship of God and performing the Spiritual and Corporal Works of Mercy. We are creatures, with only 24 hours in a day, with a single lifetime to know, love and serve God before He calls us home. Our time is not negotiable, but reminiscent of a hymn from the Liturgy of the Hours (Ref. E-13), Breviary Hymn, *"Alone with none but Thee, my God."*

"My destined time is fixed by Thee,
And Death doth know his hour.
Did warriors strong around me throng,
They could not stay his power;
No wall of stone can man defend
When Thou Thy messenger dost send."

<u>Priorities</u>

Jesus gave us the priorities by which to live in Mark 12: 28-31: ***"And one of the scribes came up and heard them disputing with one another, and seeing that He answered them well, asked Him, 'Which commandment is the first of all?'"***

"Jesus answered, 'The first is, 'Hear, O Israel: The Lord our God is one; and you shall love the Lord your God with all your heart, and with all your soul, and with all your mind, and with all your strength.'"

"The second is this, 'You shall love your neighbor as yourself.' There is no other commandment greater than these.'"

Those words are similar to the words in Matthew 22:36-40: ***"'Teacher, which is the great commandment in the law?' And He said to him, 'You shall love the Lord your God with all your heart, and with all your soul, and with all your mind. This is the great and first commandment. And a second is like it, you shall love your neighbor as yourself. On these two commandments depend all the law and the prophets.'"***

There is a common distortion in some preaching and teaching of these words, i.e., that this is all one commandment, and that there is an interchangeability between the First and Second Commandments, or even that they are identical. I believe it is a dangerous teaching, prompting confusion, and taking from God what uniquely belongs to Him. The Greek source uses the word 'deutero,' and that clearly means 'second.'

Where do ecology and environment fit?

So, given these words of Christ, where are we to fit into the text the words specifically directed to the environment and ecology? In certain Corporal Works of Mercy one can find a way of serving brothers and sisters, in Christ's name, by 'giving drink to the thirsty,' or 'feeding the hungry' with good and nourishing food. But none of that service is taught to be at the expense of, or distraction from, worshiping God. Rather, it is a manifestation of worshiping God. And that is a key point in which it is difficult to see how the overwhelming environmental and ecological concerns of Laudato Si' fit, in a deeply consistent way, into the Greatest and the Second Commandments.

That is not to say that such concerns for our environment and for the whole planet have no importance, but only that we know that their importance falls in priority below these two Great Commandments, and the challenge is to do what we can without shortchanging God, who is neither a pantheistic object nor is He willing to share His Glory in a syncretistic sense. A significant portion of environmentalism and ecology seems to be neither a Spiritual nor a Corporal Work of Mercy. It would have been helpful if Laudato Si' had addressed finding a balance, so that we do not lose sight of (or excuse any negligence in) performing our obligations or living up to our convictions.

Laudato Si' states:

"It is good for humanity and the world at large when we believers better recognize the ecological commitments which stem from our convictions." (#64)

We might add: "and we fulfill those ecological exigencies without compromising our consciences or our deepest convictions." Perhaps this is why the specific recommendations to individuals seem somewhat trite or impotent in such a long Encyclical because it is difficult at the individual level, where sin occurs and for which we will be held accountable, to identify the 'thou shalt' of Laudato Si'.

<u>Is there a position being taken against individual action, or against individualism?</u>

Pope Francis states his desire for dialogue with individuals (upon which invitation this monograph, **"Half a Dialogue,"** is offered). He states:

"...I will advance some broader proposals for dialogue and action which would involve each of us as individuals ...." (#15)

However, most of the Encyclical is really directed to action at collectivist levels, out of the hands of individuals. There seems even to be a hint that individual actions are more suspect or less trustworthy or less effective than organizational actions. Although the distinction between individual action and individualism is not clarified, the comments on 'individualism' are mostly negative, and thus biased toward the collective and away from personal freedoms.

"...romantic individualism ..." (#119)

"...rampant individualism ..." (#162)

"If we can overcome individualism, we will truly be able to develop a different lifestyle and bring about significant changes in society." (#208)

"...'myths' of a modernity grounded in a utilitarian mindset (individualism, unlimited progress, competition, consumerism, the unregulated market)." (#210)

Yet, we also remember that God knows and judges us individually, has counted the hairs of our heads, and offers a specific call to every person. Christ touched individual souls — individually! We might say He respects each 'Spiritual DNA.'

Individualism, that sense of personal challenge and commitment, that courageous willingness which steadies us rather than shaking us, that responds to God's expectations rather than to community consensus, should be much easier in a culture with protected freedoms. In oppressive cultures, perhaps, individualism is more of a risk to the person, and to the community.

When the individual meets the collective

At the fork in the road, where one direction leads to collectivist controls, rules and penalties at the highest worldly level, all administered by selected powerful sinners, or the other road where we are all sinners working out our salvation with fear and trembling in the light of God's gift to us of free will, I know I'd choose the latter.

The Implicit list of Laudato Si'?

Perhaps one reason the 'to-do' list for individuals in Laudato Si' is so short (and generally obvious) is because what is most being asked, even pressured in the Encyclical text, is hidden; i.e., yielding individual freedoms to a collective secular power. Perhaps, given the urgent timing and contrast to other reasonable and necessary priorities, it is all about preparing people to yield to such a takeover by the collective, which will command whatever is needed to 'save the planet.' But it is a wasted effort, when Christ has promised: ***"Heaven and earth will pass away, but My words will not pass away."*** (Matthew, 5:18, Mark 13:31; and Luke 21:23)

It is reminiscent of a Twilight Zone thriller, where aliens from outer space come to help the earthlings, to use their powers to make life easier, healthier, more worthwhile. The instruction book they bring with them is "To Serve Man," and the people are convinced, while they can't read all the text, that at least the title shows the good intentions of the aliens. Only after the spaceship lifts off, transporting willing earthlings disgusted with the conditions on earth to settle on a paradise planet, does the translator realize that "To Serve Man" is a cookbook.

King David himself chose a penalty of falling into the hands of a punishing God, rather than into the hands of men. In 1 Chronicles 21:13, he made his decision clear to his seer, Gad:

"Then David said to Gad, 'I am in great distress; let me fall into the hand of the Lord, for His mercy is very great; but let me not fall into the hand of man.'" It made sense to David; it makes sense to me.

<u>Psalm 118: 8-9:</u>
"It is better to take refuge in the Lord
than to put confidence in man.
It is better to take refuge in the Lord
than to put confidence in princes."

Chapter XIV
<u>Where is the Church?</u>

After I read Laudato Si' cover to cover, and made numerous notes, it became obvious, for the sake of coherent commenting, that the disparate material had to be collected and discussed under major headings; e.g. Pantheism, truth, syncretism, sustainability, subsidiarity, collectivism, action.

Even after writing about those subjects, I sensed something still lurked between the lines as unrecognized, unsaid. So I carefully re-read the entire Encyclical, as both a check on previous impressions as well as to determine if anything else should be added. During that re-reading there came a certain clarity that, indeed, it is the Church's role in both the problem and in the proposed solutions that had barely been touched in Laudato Si'. In the end, this became the most disturbing insight of all. Where is the Church, and where has she been, in the causes, the actions, and the potential cures?

The 'tipping point' in formulating these questions came in pondering the words of Laudato Si': *"Nor are there genuine ethical horizons to which one can appeal."* (*#110*) In Chapter VII, we briefly examined the role of the Church as the legitimate voice to the world, and wondered why a Catholic Encyclical would not reflect that the Church, indeed, *is* the genuine ethical horizon. This Chapter XIV expands what gave rise to such a perception, and clarifies its ramifications.

<u>Causes of concern</u>

What Laudato Si' calls *"ecological crisis"* (*#15*) is blamed variously on corporate greed, government corruption and inaction, and rampant consumerism, among other causes.

Where the Encyclical is mysteriously silent is regarding any significant role that the Church had, should have (or could have) exercised by consistently pursuing her God-given role to teach, to govern and to sanctify. It brings to mind Matthew 7:5, recounting Christ's advice: *"You hypocrite, first take the log out of your own eye, and then you will see clearly to take the speck out of your brother's eye."*

What is the Church's rightful role?

Are not greed, corruption, sloth, and serving mammon instead of God among the many sins and disturbances of soul which are subject to the Church's evangelization and preaching? If not, then we must wonder what St. Paul meant when he wrote:

"...preach the word, be urgent in season and out of season, convince, rebuke, and exhort, be unfailing in patience and in teaching. For the time is coming when people will not endure sound teaching, but having itching ears they will accumulate for themselves teachers to suit their own likings and will turn away from listening to the truth and wander into myths. As for you, always be steady, endure suffering, do the work of an evangelist, fulfill your ministry." (2 Timothy 4:2-5)

If, indeed, the Church has been deficient in these matters previously, better to admit the failure and begin anew, as after a good confession. But an Encyclical, likely to be read by relatively few, cannot replace an avid and active pulpit.

If these environmental matters are so important, why have we heard so little from preaching? Without denying any instances of relevant preaching, teaching or 'speeching' which might have occurred, anywhere in the world, it is hard to argue that the Church has had a foremost role as a key champion against any alleged demise of the world environment. If there were such importance as is now attached, where was the active involvement in prior decades? The very absence of such advocacy has an impact of its own. Whatever is not faithfully pursued, what is not taught urgently and consistently, will not receive much attention among the Faithful.

If this sounds too farfetched, we can consider the obvious absence of pulpit preaching against contraception, abortion, fornication, euthanasia and same-sex unions, just in the United States, over decades even up to the present day. Then we can understand why a majority of self-identified Catholics seem to disagree with the Church on one or more issues. Further, they may often see no difference between having an 'opinion' vs. a rightly formed conscience, if indeed one even understands the concept of a 'rightly formed conscience.'

We need look no further than paragraph #57 of Laudato Si', which words of accusation state *"...powerful financial interests prove most resistant ... and political planning tends to lack breadth of vision."* (#57)

Laudato Si' continues by asking an almost rhetorical question about the responsibility of highly powerful organizations:

"What would induce anyone, at this stage, to hold on to power only to be remembered for their inability to take action when it was urgent and necessary to do so?" (#57)

Cannot that same question be asked of the most powerful organization in the world, the one which holds the keys to the Kingdom of Heaven? Are not these words apt for self-examination, especially by Church hierarchy? How can the Church have such power and not use it? What action has the Church failed to take to prevent the present alleged crisis? What action is the Church now prepared to take, on her own initiative? What about the culpability of inaction?

Implications of action (or inaction)

While Laudato Si' rightfully denounces scarred landscapes, polluted air, contaminated water, and health impacts from toxins, and also claims there is a significant, though largely unspecified, link to the poor, one must ask (if there is a real problem): "How has the Church been trying to temper the escalation of such despoiling and to give witness that indeed there is a genuine problem and an obvious need to act?"

Beyond archiving Episcopal Conferences and writings, what 'action' has targeted relief to alleged environmental victims? And if such aid can be identified, what has worked and what has been ineffective? Where are the organizing mechanisms for such actions? How can these lessons be transferred and shared for effective implementation? How has the Church made a difference?

Is perhaps the weakness of proposals for individual action plans in Chapter XIII partly caused by long-standing inaction at various levels in the Church regarding the environment, with lack of a mobilized community and commitment to assume the challenges? Does the persistent absence of such advocacy infrastructure imply that this environmental question is only minor, and not really a relevant moral issue? If it *is* a relevant moral issue, how then can one justify inaction on one hand, but willingness, on the other hand, to yield such responsibility for a moral issue to a secular superstructure?

While Laudato Si' uses a plethora of isolated quotes from recent pontiffs, and from proceedings (Ref. E-14) of various Bishops' Conferences, such advice does not nearly equate to the clout needed to mobilize the laity, if indeed lay action had been important or necessary. Rather, it is the lack of such action which undermines the very allegation that something needs to be done NOW, and at the expense of diverting other necessary resources.   In summary, if such action were really needed, from a moral point of view, how could the Church not have been previously active? How could Church leaders now argue for oversight by a yet unformed secular mechanism, leaving its own Faithful relatively disengaged?

What priorities would now have to be realigned? Which works of mercy could or should be set aside or minimized to accommodate the work of environmental advocacy? Where is the Church's position on this moral battlefield?

The historic model of action

If *"ecological conversion"* (*#217, #219, #220, e.g.*) is now deemed to be so important, how is the Church encouraging and training its members to respond to such need?   Or publicizing the opportunity to serve? A key question is: "Will actions by the Faithful on their own initiative be aided or impeded by actions or inactions of the Church?"

The tradition of the Church for centuries had been to act on her own, e.g. to open and run orphanages, soup kitchens, schools and colleges, hospitals and nursing homes, providing direct service to the needy. Many of those services are now abandoned, the people served dispersed to secular providers. Will advocating governmental superstructure repeat that cycle?

The mechanism with which to respond is weak, and more easily cedes its rightful place to government regulation, especially to governments opposed to Freedom of Religion, as in the closing of some Catholic adoption agencies for their lack of willingness to refer to same-sex couples, and impairment of spiritual services to veterans. Virtually the only serving arm still owned and operated by the Church, substantially untouched by hostile government, is the Catholic Cemetery, which is not a highly actionable resource.

As the Church has become more of a 'middleman distributor' of financial resources to organizations which function outside the Church's direct control, the link of the Faithful to the work itself is seriously weakened and unfocused. Recipient organizations (such as reported for the Catholic Campaign for Human Development and on occasion for Catholic Relief Services) are sometimes accused of flouting Catholic Teaching in the way they disburse funds.

Money, not action and service, has become the medium of exchange, inside as well as outside the Church. And the Faithful may, thus, reasonably determine that they can distribute their own financial resources better than the United States Conference of Catholic Bishops and its allied organizations. One sadly neglected point in understanding the demise of the pew population is just how much these organizational and volunteer services in the Church once wove tighter the fabric of Catholic community.

Are there cures?

Laudato Si' sets forth a few individual action points; most are listed in Chapter XIII. Unfortunately, sometimes the Encyclical dismisses individual effort and at other times seems to weakly acknowledge its benefit. But recommendations for project implementation by the Church, among the Magisterium and Faithful in the pew, are substantially absent from the Encyclical, as if all the fixes are mandated to come from ceding authority and resources to forces outside the Church.

Yet, there are several areas where direct services could be created anew, or revitalized, where there is need and could strengthen unity and cohesion. Unity will become increasingly important in resisting adverse secular forces, such as mandated physician-assisted suicide. Hopefully, such situations are being appropriately reviewed, and opportunities timely considered.

Power and Money

Many excerpted Encyclical quotes involve finances or power or both (even in *"A Christian Prayer in Unity with Creation"* mentioned in the next chapter.) The apparent obsession in Laudato Si' with power and money is unfortunate, as these are not the charisms needed for the Church's mission to change hearts and save souls. There is an absence in the Encyclical of noting the Church's obligation to facilitate deep conversion, which is more vital than behavior modification. Ecological conversion is not the same as metanoia of soul.

The Encyclical's emphasis is on world-power reorganization, creating a secular power super-structure, forcing certain actions or penalties, transferring money or exercising authority to limit growth or to execute the ambiguous and dangerous concept of 'sustainability.' Regrettably, all of these matters now seem to have the apparent 'endorsement' of the Holy See.

Questionable Alignments

It is particularly disturbing to those in the pews when proposals and examples at such high levels show alignment with what even the most simple soul knows to be antithetical to long-standing Church teaching; e.g. improper advocacy of collectivist power and oversight, embracing the dangerous United Nations sustainability language, and failure to strongly differentiate Catholic Teaching from any coincidental overlap of minor or temporary goals. Mincing words is not in the tradition of Sts. Thomas More, Edmund Campion, Oscar Romero or Charles Lwanga, nor is avoiding risk in the tradition of Sts. Perpetua and Felicity, Isaac Jogues, Maximilian Kolbe or Edith Stein, or of so many other Christians and nameless martyrs killed for the Faith, not for cleaning up a waste dump. Ironically, we already know the saints we need to learn from for survival of souls in this new, ever old, secular order.

It isn't too difficult to demonstrate that people do want their lives to have meaning, to be inspired, to serve truly higher purposes, and not to settle for less than the most they have been called to do. Certainly it is reasonable for us to look to the words of Jesus in determining what is important, and what is not. We want to inherit the world which He promised to make new, but let's have no illusions that we will create it ourselves!

Risky language implications

Another foreboding concern is caused by the confusing language of Laudato Si', which portends great risk from future actions by powerful governments. The Laudato Si' words lend themselves to being twisted and used against Catholics. It is not too great a stretch to imagine that the words *"the firm resolve to achieve sustainability"* (#207) written by the Vicar of Christ might be interpreted in the future as a 'Catholic approval' to use whatever means necessary to reduce population, even though that was not explicitly written as such, and even though Church Teaching clearly rejects the human depopulation strategies of sustainability.

As children we knew and understood the words: "Show me your friends and I'll tell you who you are." The liaisons formed between those with power in the Church and the advocates of the secular world who mean different things from the same words are too dangerous to be ignored. Movement down that slippery slope toward sinful implementation of a sustainability program is reflected even in Laudato Si's words:

"...the idea of infinite or unlimited growth, which proves so attractive to economists, financiers and experts in technology ... is based on the lie that there is an infinite supply of the earth's goods, and this leads to the planet being squeezed dry beyond every limit." (#106)

The implicit assumption of the cited criticism is that the earth does not have the resources to care for the people. Translation: God has not and will not take care of His creation. Thus the groundwork is laid to restrict resources, withhold life support or implement onerous family controls or refuse medical care to the elderly and infirm, or to victims of disease or disasters.

However, such fears need to be examined in the context of Sacred Scripture, and the command to be fruitful and multiply. One manifestation that the Word is indeed from God is how, over 2000 years, it is still just as relevant today, and that we are given what we need to live a moral and spiritual life. The world may have changed, from sending runners on foot to deliver messages to modern high-speed satellite communications, but what matters in the bible is unchanged. It would be surprising, therefore, to have the world multiply itself into over-population disaster, without any warning of such an impending fate.

Bleak tone

Laudato Si' paints a bleak picture of the current and future world environment. The issue of tone is disappointing since, if the Church can't witness to joy, who can? It is not about whether there is cause for sadness; rather, the sadness seems almost despairing; e.g., Laudato Si' uses the expressions:

"...a sort of mental pollution." (#47)

"...a deep and melancholic dissatisfaction with interpersonal relations, or a harmful sense of isolation...." (#47)

"...humanity has changed profoundly ...." (#113)

"...to recover the values and the great goals swept away by our unrestrained delusions of grandeur." (#114)

"An inadequate presentation of Christian anthropology gave rise to a wrong understanding of the relationship between human beings and the world." (#116) An inadequate presentation by whom? How will it be rectified? Will the error of claiming over-population be corrected?

"...constant schizophrenia, wherein a technocracy which sees no intrinsic value in lesser beings coexists with the other extreme, which sees no special value in human beings." (#118) Using the medical diagnostic word 'schizophrenia' seems unfair to those with that mental disorder.

The point is not to criticize any justifiable complaints or indictments of what needs to be changed, but rather to notice a thread of hopeless tone, sans responsibility or expectation, which asserts itself within the framework of dialogue in the Encyclical. What seems missing is the vision of relevant change, in cooperation with God's Teaching, which exhorts but respects the free will of mankind. Credibility is worsened by favoring the unproven 'global warming,' and opposing air conditioning and fossil fuels, yet implying a link to Church Teaching, intimidating the less technically cognizant. There is a conflict between proposed rule by a designated global institution and the potential impact on the dignity of the individual, disregarding the principle of subsidiarity.

"Every violation of solidarity and civic friendship harms the environment ... institutions develop to regulate human relationships. Anything which weakens those institutions has negative consequences, such as injustice, violence and loss of freedom." (#142) It is not an obligation of being human to agree with and support all artificially established institutions. It is disappointing that the words of Laudato Si' weren't qualified by the assertion of and respect for free will and self-government — of the people, by the people and for the people.

<u>**Where is the Catholic Church?**</u>

One inevitably is compelled to ask: "Where is the Catholic Church in these concerns, other than in an Encyclical?" Many other parties are blamed for the secular obsessions and consumerist hunger, but barely touched is where is the Church to be found — in the battle for souls or in an environmental skirmish? If the Church cannot teach what is necessary in ethics and morals, who can? And why would the Church willingly give up her role to secular forces and human organizations? Advocacy for the environment should be more clearly subservient to Faith and to the salvation of souls.

Laudato Si' fails to clearly define Catholic life principles, using instead shifting concepts and references like "sustainability," rather than unabashed Church Teaching. Although Laudato Si' is addressed to the whole world, it seriously misses the opportunity to evangelize that world. The 'Catholic' message, to the world and also to the Faithful, is sadly diluted.

It is the Church's mission to draw souls to Jesus, Who fills and sustains those who seek Him. The Church has a unique advantage in being able to work across borders, which governments and secular organizations cannot do as effectively. Should not the Church clarify her role to Christ's priorities, rather than transfer power to the United Nations or to collectivist overseers? Rather than imposing behavioral changes? or delegating her charitable works to the secular?

<u>**Did the hierarchy miss the mission?**</u>

Reading this Encyclical was a deeply sad experience, not because science and technology seem condemned as the enemy, or even because distorted science is accepted, but because of what the Church has failed to do. Where is there even a nod to the Greatest Commandment?   And where are we called to intense gratitude for the gifts God has given us, and for our privilege to use them, or to atone for misusing them?

Rather, the Encyclical reflects the dullness and aching of a world not turned to Christ. The readers have a right to look for some hope and joy. Can we even be Catholic without hope? The most pristine external world will not create hope. And if we have hope, how can we not have joy?

If there were serious reasons to expect the Faithful to hoist the flag of environmental commitment, then one must ask where are the rehabilitative changes needed on the part of the 'business' of Church, i.e. its own 'to-do' list on behalf of the environment and ecology?

Conclusion

The simplicity of the conclusion of this chapter is this: if these environmental issues are so important that the priority of an Encyclical is brought to bear, where has the Church been while the degradation was occurring? And, why? How then, do we now argue that environmental activism is suddenly so important that other priorities would have to be set aside? Which priorities and at what cost is never specified. And what would the impact of such deferral be on souls needing to be served and on those souls charged with serving them?

What perhaps makes more sense is that what has not been of great priority or urgency previously, in the judgment of prior pontiffs and the sense of the Faithful, should not now trump traditional Church Teaching or the good of souls. Laudato Si' is not a work like Pope Saint John Paul II's "Theology of the Body," with deep spiritual effect; so, great care is needed in any implementation, in anything which draws people away from the Creator toward the created.

Chapter XV
<u>Disturbing Prayers</u>

It is not within my ability or privilege to comment on strengths or weaknesses in any particular prayers, as prayers per se, and certainly not regarding prayers promulgated by the Holy Father. How can I know what prayers please Almighty God and which don't? But I do sense what makes me uncomfortable, and sometimes the reasons for the discomfort. And I am willing to share those reactions.

<u>Concerns about the new environmental prayers</u>

Since Pope Francis solicited dialogue in Laudato Si', and included two prayers in particular at the end of the Encyclical, it seems fair and necessary to comment on them. And 'disturbing' is an appropriate word. After 2000 years of the Catholic Church's using prayers for so many varying needs, it seems a bit strange that we don't already have prayers for virtually everything of importance, and that we actually need 'new prayers' for ecology and the environment. Therefore, it is meaningful to compare the newly proposed prayers to those to which we are accustomed. The more traditional prayers evoke the understanding of praise 'by' the environment, whereas the latest proposed prayers seem to be prayers 'for' the environment, somewhat inconsistent with our usual practice.

Is there any better exemplar of prayer 'by' the environment than the Canticle of Daniel in the Liturgy of the Hours? This Morning Prayer (Lauds) is one of praise, offered worldwide from the Psalter (First and Third Sundays) and used on many Solemnities and Feast Days as well. One might consider it a kind of 'premier' canticle due to such prominence and unabashed praise of God, especially from the fiery furnace.

<u>**Comparison of Canticle of Daniel 3:57-88, 56 (Universalis on-line version) to the first new prayer in Laudato Si'**</u>

<u>Canticle of Daniel</u>

Bless the Lord, all His works, praise and exalt Him for ever.
Bless the Lord, you heavens; all His angels, bless the Lord.

Bless the Lord, you waters above the heavens;
　　　　all His powers, bless the Lord.
Bless the Lord, sun and moon; all stars of the sky, bless the Lord.

Bless the Lord, rain and dew; all you winds, bless the Lord.
Bless the Lord, fire and heat; cold and warmth, bless the Lord.

Bless the Lord, dew and frost; ice and cold, bless the Lord.
Bless the Lord, ice and snow; day and night, bless the Lord.

Bless the Lord, light and darkness;
　　　　lightning and storm-clouds, bless the Lord.
Bless the Lord, all the earth, praise and exalt Him for ever.

Bless the Lord, mountains and hills;
　　　　all growing things, bless the Lord.
Bless the Lord, seas and rivers;
　　　　springs and fountains, bless the Lord.

Bless the Lord, whales and fish; birds of the air, bless the Lord.
Bless the Lord, wild beasts and tame; sons of men, bless the Lord.

Bless the Lord, O Israel, praise and exalt Him for ever.
Bless the Lord, His priests, all His servants, bless the Lord.

Bless the Lord, spirits and souls of the just;
　　　　all who are holy and humble, bless the Lord.
　　　　Ananias, Azarias, Mishael, bless the Lord,
　　　　praise and exalt Him for ever.

Let us bless Father, Son and Holy Spirit,
　　　　praise and exalt Them for ever.
Bless the Lord in the firmament of heaven,
　　　　praise and glorify Him for ever.

<u>A prayer for our earth by Pope Francis</u>
(intended for all who believe in a Creator God)

"All-powerful God, you are present in the whole universe and in the smallest of your creatures. You embrace with your tenderness all that exists. Pour out upon us the power of your love, that we may protect life and beauty. Fill us with peace, that we may live as brothers and sisters, harming no one.

"O God of the poor, help us to rescue the abandoned and forgotten of this earth, so precious in your eyes. Bring healing to our lives, that we may protect the world and not prey on it, that we may sow beauty, not pollution and destruction.

"Touch the hearts of those who look only for gain at the expense of the poor and the earth. Teach us to discover the worth of each thing, to be filled with awe and contemplation, to recognize that we are profoundly united with every creature as we journey towards your infinite light.

"We thank you for being with us each day. Encourage us, we pray, in our struggle for justice, love and peace." (#246)

<u>Comparison</u>

The Canticle of Daniel is deeply oriented to praising the Lord; but "A prayer for our earth" is just that – a prayer 'for' the earth, not 'by' the earth in praise of God, and includes a 'to-do' list for what God should do about those who are not living in the spirit of the prayer that is being offered. Even in the Canticle of Daniel, the three young men in the furnace are not praying for themselves but calling on the whole world to praise God, no matter what He does with them or about the fire. This dichotomy between prayer 'by' and prayer 'for' the environment underlies my discomfort with the new prayer, which personally I find challenging to pray.

Lest anyone think that the Canticle of Daniel is pantheistic, it is not. St. Francis used this approach when he personalized "Mother Earth," in a poetic praise of God. To personalize the spirit of any part of creation, as being purposed for the Glory of God, is not the same as claiming that God is actually the element of His Creation.

A Christian prayer in union with creation by Pope Francis

The second prayer given in Laudato Si', offered for use by all Christians, is *"A Christian Prayer in Union with Creation."* Rather than reproducing here the entire second prayer, which is readily available on line, and belaboring similar concerns, there are a few verses within the prayer which call for special focus. For example:

"Holy Spirit, by your light you guide this world towards the Father's love and accompany creation as it groans in travail." (#246)

That verse relates to Romans 8:22, in which St. Paul says: ***"We know that the whole creation has been groaning in travail together until now;"*** but the scriptural message seems to be more one of waiting for adoption as full sons of God, rather than intended to attribute the groanings of all creation to pollution or environmental problems. I would hope that all translators are being very careful not to use the environment as a spear of eisegesis into the text of Holy Scripture.

The plea *"help us to protect all life"* raises serious questions about past and current commitments to defend life in the womb, to resist euthanasia, to refuse to accommodate the contraceptive culture, to oppose gender selection and gender mutilation, to remedy human trafficking. Reading a prayer specifically related to the environment, without overt reference to so many other attacks on life, one wonders how many of our deeper priorities are consequentially being excluded.

Conversely, those words *"in union with creation"* raise the questions: "Where are these more important issues of life itself, and of intrinsic evil, being raised and opposed? What merits entire encyclicals when other, more vital subjects, seem almost ignored?" One cannot simply look at the Teaching Office of the Church and argue that something has been taught for nearly 2000 years, and that is 'enough.' The need is today, and so should be the teaching, in my opinion — not 'new' teaching, but reverberation of all that the Body of Christ has known and followed for millennia.

Another concern experienced while reading this particular prayer of Pope Francis is that a certain gentleness and uplifting language in that prayerful writing is awkwardly contrasted to language that is more harsh, alienating or even divisive. It seems rooted in an artificial division between rich and poor.

Yet, as we know and as Pope Francis pointed out (#226) Christ looked upon the rich young man and ***"loved him."*** (Mark 10:21) Perhaps looking with love on those who are 'rich' would be more efficacious for change, than a tone of chiding? More honoring of free will? And of Christian unity?

Some would find it very difficult to say (or to hear said at daily Mass, where parishioners offer intercessions,) these words from *"A Christian Prayer in Union with Creation"*:

"Enlighten those who possess power and money that they may avoid the sin of indifference, that they may love

the common good, advance the weak, and care for this world in which we live." (#246) or

'Touch the hearts of those who look only for gain at the expense of the poor and the earth." (#246)

I personally would feel such a petition to be inappropriate for offering by an attendee at daily Mass. We are told it isn't right to seek to remove the splinter in the eye of another when we have a log in our own. ***"Or how can you say to your brother, 'Let me take the speck out of your eye,' when there is the log in your own eye?"*** (Matthew 7:4) Perhaps this is part of the reason for discomfort with this particular prayer? Why are those who possess power and money so selectively targeted in prayers of paragraph #246, when all people should be avoiding the *"sin of indifference?"* And when all people are sinners?

One example of a log in the eye (a big log!) is when dioceses close the churches in the inner cities, meant to offer the greatest riches in the world, the Gospel, to all people. How are the poor not being disproportionately excluded, especially when they lack transportation to reach a suburban alternative?

Moreover, let us also consider that the opposite words would also be distasteful and inappropriate for intercessions at Mass; i.e. *"We give Thee thanks for all those who possess power and money and have avoided the sin of indifference, loved the common good, advanced the weak, and cared for this world in which we live."* Either type of language seems needlessly divisive, picking and choosing for selected vices or virtues.

As is stated in Luke 17:10: ***"So you also, when you have done all that is commanded you, say, 'We are unworthy servants; we have only done what was our duty.'"***

<u>**Underdeveloped link between poor and the environment**</u>

While the link between the poor and the environment is stated repeatedly in Laudato Si', the explanation or development of the linkage is weak. An example would be the words in the 'Christian'-oriented prayer of Pope Francis: *"The poor and the earth are crying out." (#246)* Although it repeats the theme which underlies the Encyclical, it is still a non sequitur, an unequal yoking, with the case for cause and effect not made. The repetition has an uncomfortable sense of rote prayer to condition the acceptance of a connection. Another example is:

"The exploitation of the planet has already exceeded acceptable limits and we still have not solved the problem of poverty." (#27) **"The poor you always have with you..."** (John 12:8) was stated by Christ. Such words are also contained in Matthew 26:11 and Mark 14:7. Can we reasonably expect to 'solve' the problem of poverty through interventions based on governmental power? Should we even act as if we can do so? And how does *"exploitation of the planet"* relate to not solving other problems?

Individual acts of charity arise in the heart, and God uses those for the shaping of souls, of both the giver and the recipient. Governments die at the end of time; only people are judged, one by one, at the Particular Judgment. Interfering with the ability of individual souls to serve God through the Corporal and Spiritual Works of Mercy, by stripping their resources to do so, is another concern worth pondering and re-considering.

"And so the day of rest, centered on the Eucharist, sheds it [sic] light on the whole week, and motivates us to greater concern for nature and the poor." (#237)

This is another sentence which is difficult to understand as cause and effect, since the Eucharist, the Sacrament of Love, motivates us (and obligates us) to share a self-sacrificing love with all peoples, rich or poor. We are also called to serve with many actions, such as the Spiritual Works of Mercy, not limiting our motivations only to nature and the poor, both undefined terms in the Encyclical. If we look to the Gospels and Christ's own words, it is difficult to find any connection between the poor and either nature or the environment.

Jesus does seem, through the 'purse,' to have provided something for the poor, as implied at the Last Supper in the words of John 13:29: *"Some thought that, because Judas had the money box, Jesus was telling him, 'Buy what we need for the feast'; or, that he should give something to the poor."*

We particularly notice in the Gospels that Christ condemned stinginess and insensitivity on the part of the rich man who ignored the starving Lazarus at his gate (Luke, Chapter 16.) We also see that Christ personally and often responded to those in need, whether at the Wedding Feast of Cana, raising the dead, feeding with loaves and fish, or curing lepers and demoniacs, among His other works. He had great compassion for those in front of Him who were in desperate situations.

But He, Who had all power in His Hands, apparently didn't make poor people rich in what didn't matter to their souls, or which absence gave those who lacked resources a unique ability to glorify God in ways that those with more power or money struggle to do, i.e. who *"give out of their abundance"* rather than out of poverty. (Luke 21:4) No, the message Jesus sent to John the Baptist in prison was not *"...the poor are made rich"* but rather *"...the poor have good news preached to them."* (Matthew 11:5)

This charity, sharing the Word of God, exceeds all other charities, which is why evangelizing and witnessing to our Faith are so essential.

It is a great disappointment that an Encyclical of more than 40,000 words, asserting the linkage of the poor and the environment, gives so little attention to preaching the 'good news' in that context. We must all beware of being covetous of what other people have, and rather be covetous for the sake of souls that all may better know, love and serve God.

<u>For what should we pray?</u>

Jesus also did not act to interfere with the Roman occupation and persecution of the Jewish people. For He said in Matthew 10:28: ***"And do not fear those who kill the body but cannot kill the soul; rather fear Him who can destroy both soul and body in hell."***

What a tragedy it is that the real persecution in the world, of Christians for their faith, and of the destruction of babies in the womb, is virtually ignored compared to such great focus on weather, climate, pollution and its effects. Even if global warming and climate change were true, a combination of acts of God and man-made factors, it is perhaps appropriate to be suffered as a call to the world for repentance and atonement.

The myth that humanity can act to change the weather or climate is an affront to the powers of God. Simply reduce a fossil fuel or two, move money from one pocket to another, and God's judgment can be avoided? Not too many more foolish plans have been created in world history.

A better prayer might be that God will relent on the destruction which He has every right to impose. Rather, acting as if governments, in their own power, can impose rules to change global temperatures and weather effects just adds to the scandal of false belief. And when supported by any church's teaching it adds to the alienation. What an even greater tragedy if the Catholic Church were to be involved in endorsing or leading such a perception. It is not easy to ignore the extensive scriptural writings in which God asserts His complete power over weather and climate. His control would still be true even if Scripture did not mention His power. But perhaps one of the reasons for those writings is for us, *"for such a time as this,"* as Mordecai said to Queen Esther (in Esther 4:14), regarding the urgency of speaking Truth to Power, even at great risk.

The ultimate tragedy would be if the world were engaged in such wasteful and presumptuous efforts while *"eating and drinking, marrying and giving in marriage"* (Matthew 24:38), not only at the expense of the time, effort and resources used, but especially instead of focusing on repentance, before there became no time to repent. Now that is something deserving of prayer!

While we do not know the day or the hour, we do have reason from Revelation to expect that the natural world will be ravaged. There is no need to quote extensively here, but perhaps just to note the results of the preliminary onslaught from Revelation 8:7b: *"...and a third of the earth was burnt up, and a third of the trees were burnt up, and all green grass was burnt up."*

Chapter XVI
<u>Dear Pope Francis,</u>

Perhaps the best way to summarize this monograph is to return to the original intention, to write a "Dear Pope Francis" letter, highlighting conclusions from the foregoing chapters, always with the intention to be in the spirit of dialogue, which is what Pope Francis invited.

Dear Pope Francis,

Thank you for your invitation to engage with you in dialogue regarding your Encyclical, Laudato Si'. For that purpose I have entitled this work **"Half a Dialogue."** I am only able to set forth my own reactions, beliefs and opinions, trusting that your invitation is genuine and that my responsibility is to reply with truth, as best it is given me to understand.

While I have tried to respond in that context and spirit, I make no claim to adequacy, let alone perfection. I simply reaffirm that I have done the best I am able, and ask your patience as I set forth my concerns about Laudato Si', detailed in 15 chapters of this monograph. Please do understand that I am limited by needing to work with the English translation, which I must take as being faithful to your work and to your intent.

<u>Organization of the monograph</u>

I have fully read the Encyclical twice, with care and diligence and prayer, and some sections many more times than twice. From the monograph you will see that I have not tracked my reply 'section by section' of the Encyclical, but rather developed macro subjects for attention and communication. So I will only comment in this letter in a broad sense, as the detail is set forth in the various chapters of **"Half a Dialogue"** and needs only a little repetition.

In the **Foreword**, I offered my belief and understanding as to why such a reply is permissible. I also addressed the question of infallibility in Chapter XII. The **Introduction** describes the triggering issue of my being interested in Laudato Si', as I am unconvinced (as a scientist) of the claims of 'global warming' and 'climate change.' In the **Overview** chapter are words of orientation and perspective regarding **"Half a Dialogue."** This monograph seeks to be received as part of a dialogue, especially regarding the following ten concerns.

A. Scientific truth vs. 'global-warming' allegations

I was first drawn to read Laudato Si' because of concern that the Church had taken sides in a scientific debate, a debate which lacks information to prove or to disprove either premise. It is an issue in which consensus has no meaning at all, except for political purposes. The debate is likely to continue for some time but, eventually, the truth should be known, as it was in the Galileo affair. Even if truly scientific results were eventually to 'prove' a 'global-warming' phenomenon, it would only have been a correct 'guess' without having first had proof, but still a violation of the methods of science.

When I first heard that Your Holiness was going to accept the allegations regarding 'global warming,' I must admit I cringed, and still do, remembering how embarrassed the Church has been for centuries over Pope Urban VIII's support for the arguments that the earth is the center of the universe. I do fear similar loss of credibility could be occurring again, in a most technological of ages, in the haste to align with and embrace political claims regarding 'global warming.' Moreover, it seems particularly mortifying not only to have merely made a mistaken conclusion, but to have written also extensively in the

Encyclical in specific rejection of Science and Technology, the very ground on which Truth should be able to stand. In some sense, the Encyclical opposes Truth, being proudly closed to it.

I find it to be sadly relevant, however, that virtually all the claims in Laudato Si' of a scientific nature, beginning with the very allegation of 'global warming' itself, are unsupported by footnotes or other references, while the writings of popes, bishops and earth conferences are highly referenced, and some of those opinions stated as fact. The irony of the position taken by Laudato Si', for all its negativity toward technology and science, is that the Encyclical chooses a poor, inadequate, and even undisclosed scientific hypothesis as the argument on which to make its stand, and ignores the valid debate which rages around the issue.

We would not argue for presenting Theology in such a way; neither, I believe, is it appropriate to accept rumors or opinions regarding science in such a way. Such dichotomy alienates rather than unites. It is particularly disturbing that the Catholic Church, which has championed the scientific method, now defects to the allegations of secular forces, calling the scientific method *"...a technique of possession, mastery and transformation ... as if the subject were to find itself in the presence of something formless, completely open to manipulation."* (#106)

I do wish that Laudato Si' had been written only with deep concern for the environment, without ever having risked aligning with governments, politicians, or the United Nations in its lobby for 'global warming' with pseudo-science. I fear that Catholic credibility, so badly needed in a devolving secular world, is further endangered and damaged. Moreover, engaging in the geo-political cause of 'global warming,' the Church herself risks compromising Truth on some of the most basic issues, perhaps even being boxed into untenable positions.

While it is true that dialogue has been invited regarding the Encyclical, what that invitation lacks is encouragement to disagree on the matter of 'global warming,' per se. That becomes a founding premise of the Encyclical, even challenging the honor of those who would disagree. However, to the extent that one may disagree, and I believe we may, I take this opportunity to do so, not because 'global warming' has been proved untrue, but because it hasn't been proved true. And actions and programs, directed to the cure of something that may not be real, risks damaging even more by reallocating crucial resources to the less important, with a concomitant loss of reputation and credibility.

It seems a contradiction to argue to be stewards of the environment but not be stewards of truth, which can neither be reached through consensus, nor by suppressing those who would disagree. As Eve found, a half-truth is worse than an outright lie, because it misleads through the masquerade of truth. Scientific truth is not the enemy. Until a matter is proved (or is acknowledged to be a matter of Faith), an open mind should keep, well, an open mind. I think the Encyclical lacks balance on matters unproven, and lacks respect for the achievements of scientists of good intentions, over millennia.

Although "Scientific truth vs. global-warming allegations" is only point #1 of 10 points, nevertheless it is one of the most important, impairing what should be inherent truth in all points, and reopening old wounds from the claim of geocentrism versus heliocentrism of the universe.

B. Environmentalism, Pantheism and 'One World Religion'

The ever present threat of 'wars and rumors of wars' reminds us of the fragility of peace, the unfulfilled desire of the human heart for peace, and the vulnerability of humanity to promises of peace. Perhaps the human race has never been more susceptible than now to the hunger for peace, as war threatens to tear cultures apart and wrench Christianity from its Middle Eastern womb. It becomes almost a relief to focus on environmentalism – how can anyone disagree with making the world a 'nicer, cleaner' place? But in reading Laudato Si', I did not come away with the sense that the world was going to be 'improved'; rather that care for the environment, a good thing in itself, could bring us to a kind of Pantheism, into the secret machinations of founding 'One World Religion' based on a 'New World Evangelization.'

The idea that nature can unite us, and be a source of peace could easily tempt its advocates to support the idea of 'One World Religion,' based on environmentalism, sans dogma, doctrine or anything else which divides. The unproven threat of 'global warming' and 'climate change,' positioned as the purported and unchallenged common enemy of mankind, has the potential to unite people in pursuit of a new, common creed of Babel, a gateway to a singular, environmental 'religion.' How can we ignore that particular threat in the ever-rising tide of secularism, which lauds permission to sin against foundational moral truth? How can we evangelize the true and perfect order of God's Revelation against the entropy of the slippery slope, if we stand with even one foot on an environmental creed?   I am particularly concerned that the words of Laudato Si' do not anticipate the reality of such risks.

Moreover, it becomes particularly alluring when a religious leader, especially Your Holiness, takes a prominent role in promoting such ecological directives within the context of Faith. The pantheistic 'groves' and 'high places' of worship in the Old Testament remind us how easily human hearts are led astray, undermining the true place of God by adoring what He created, instead of the Creator Himself. Such human weaknesses still assail and divert, raising the created to much too high a position relative to the priorities Christ taught us, including the need for humility in our own humanity. A mindset of self-sufficient idolatry, it would seem, can only dilute efforts of the righteous labor of love to give praise and glory to God!

It seems that such environmental language, bordering on worship, will be confusing to the Catholic in the pew, and open up possibilities of unknowingly embracing pantheistic practices, leading to de facto idolatry, even without full assent or understanding the implications. The concern is not for governments or organizations, but for 'the little ones,' my brothers and sisters, that they may not be led astray. The energy, effort and attention in propagating a creed of environmentalism risks establishing a false Gospel, and crippling efforts to grow in the True Faith. Jesus charges us to **"first sit down and count the cost,"** in Luke 14:28-32. Thus, is it not a valid question to ask what costs might be incurred due to such environmental emphasis? What opportunities lost?

Some of the words of the Encyclical are already consistent with Pantheism or pantheistic tendencies. One of the most frightening quotations which I read in Laudato Si' is in Paragraph #160: *"Leaving an inhabitable planet to future generations is, first and foremost, up to us. The issue is one which dramatically affects us, for it has to do with the ultimate meaning of our earthly sojourn."*

With all due respect, Your Holiness, as Catholics we know that the "ultimate meaning of our earthly sojourn" is to know, love and serve God, and to be united with Him for all eternity, and NOT to run an improvement program for the planet. Christ said **"Heaven and Earth will pass away, but My words will not pass away."** (Matthew 24:35, Mark 13:31 and Luke 21:33) And from Revelation we also read that the planet, however pristine, will not survive end times, but we will. Forever.

C. Syncretism is an abuse of True Faith

Frightening as is the 'deity' of environmentalism, leading to Pantheism, even more disturbing are the words used in Laudato Si' to effect the synthesis of the environmental and the holy, creating a potentially syncretistic path. The perception of Pantheism, as noted in the preceding section, and the risk of its being used toward 'One World Religion,' is further validated by an emerging scenario of syncretism.

If I may, please, I call your attention to words taken from the Christian Faith but being used in a whole new and confusing context in Laudato Si': *conversion, communion, sacrament, sins, spiritual, spirituality, sacred, sacredness, sanctified, mystery, trinitarian dynamism, trinitarian key, supernatural, repent, pilgrimage, covenant, and as a path to offering ourselves as a "living sacrifice, holy and acceptable"* and more!

I regret needing to say that using these words, holy and sacred as they are to Catholics, cannot but draw us into seeing environmentalism as a worship path acceptable to God. Quite frankly, there is no leader in the entire world who could do more damage to the faith of the little ones with these words than our own Holy Father, by legitimizing such language. And it is deeply disappointing and frightening to need to say so. I beg you not to promulgate such combinations of environmental matters with words which Catholics consider holy in the faith, lest, through rote use, we misunderstand and are led into sin.

D. The risk of alignment to 'sustainability' speech

I believe there is a serious risk in aligning with the United Nations 'sustainability' language, which has been defined by some supporters in themes as radical as a need to reduce world population from 7 billion to 1 billion. I wish it had been said clearly in Laudato Si' that any of the apparent strategies aimed at achieving population reduction are in violation of Catholic Teaching. It would have been helpful to have had stronger statements on Catholic morality regarding such issues as contraception, abortion, euthanasia and, even, infertile by nature, 'same-sex unions.'

'Sustainability' words are used 27x in the Encyclical, raising an appearance of cooperation with a highly suspect global agenda. I am deeply concerned that excerpts will be used in the future to deliberately misstate or misuse a sentence such as in paragraph #207: *"Let ours be a time remembered for the awakening of a new reverence for life, the firm resolve to achieve sustainability, the quickening of the struggle for justice and peace, and the joyful celebration of life."* Unfortunately, it seems inevitable that the papal words *"the firm resolve to achieve sustainability"* will become misleading in the future, and taken for the Church's having endorsed the now current meaning of 'sustainability.'

Of similar concern is Laudato Si's endorsement of the sustainability argument:

"...the idea of infinite or unlimited growth, which proves so attractive to economists, financiers and experts in technology ... is based on the lie that there is an infinite supply of the earth's goods, and this leads to the planet being squeezed dry beyond every limit." (#106)

A *"squeezed dry"* planet sounds like one more argument on behalf of those who want to reduce population, and it is very surprising to find those words in Laudato Si'. Again, this is a subject of much on-going, genuine debate, in which it now appears that Your Holiness has unfortunately taken sides. The implicit assumption is that God has not given the earth sufficient resources to care for its people. Such an assumption lays the groundwork to justify the requirement of one-child or no-child families, to refuse medical care to the elderly and infirm, and to neglect victims of epidemics or natural disasters.

It is disappointing that all this mention of 'sustainability,' and the errors it promulgates, isn't refuted by a stronger statement of morality, and condemnation of those actions (Ref. E-15) which violate human dignity, such as using financial pressure on sovereign countries to encourage immoral practices. (The allegation that a tetanus vaccine provided to Kenya is modified to be contraceptive is under investigation as we go to press.)

The language of 'sustainability' is embraced by the Catholic Church only at great risk, and potential scandal. I believe it would have been wiser to use an alternative word, and also to have used the global ambo more powerfully to teach the world the non-negotiable expectations of population morality.

E. Subsidiarity--unsupported as a basic Catholic principle

It is unfortunate that the basic Catholic principle of subsidiarity is only mentioned twice in Laudato Si', because without that principle, strategic implementation inevitably tends toward collectivism. Especially telling was the quotation from Pope Benedict's Encyclical, Caritas in Veritate, containing his speech to the United Nations. The quotation is out of context, and the specific reference to subsidiarity is twice avoided.

I believe the fundamental principle of subsidiarity should also have been rigorously applied in the Encyclical to its very questionable recommendations of collectivism. The spirit of empowering at the lowest possible level, in respect of the Almighty's trust in humankind and His gift of free will, is effectively ignored in Laudato Si' by its repeated calls for a kind of superstructure decision-making entity, empowered to even penalize sovereign powers. The Encyclical seems to surrender this long-standing Catholic principle of subsidiarity to the exigencies of supposed effectiveness, but without explanation or defense.

It may be difficult to consistently apply the principle of subsidiarity to every situation, yet I believe the dignity of human beings is worth the effort.

F. Collectivism and covetousness

There seems to be a departure from prior papal teachings with respect to collectivism. If that is not so, if I have misunderstood, then I wish that a clear explanation of why it is not socialistic would have been furnished. Otherwise the Encyclical's advocating actions against sovereign nations and proposing high-level oversight with power to punish does seem socialistic in practice, and difficult to justify from a human rights point of view. Furthermore, writings of Pope Benedict XVI (Cardinal Ratzinger) regarding Liberation Theology do not seem to be acknowledged, respected or reiterated in the premises of Laudato Si'.

One particularly disturbing aspect of the Encyclical is the desired redistribution of wealth. Not only is it of concern from a political viewpoint, but also seems, in practice, to violate the 10th Commandment, by coveting finances, power and resources of other sovereign countries, and by diminishing their sovereignty with intrusive and divisive 'new structures.' Even private property rights are targeted, the will of sovereign nations ignored, and undermining of world capital structure risked. An underlying fallacy, in my opinion, is the assumption that those wanting to impose or manage such a new world order have the ability to act from a sense of righteousness generally unseen in the hearts of men. John 2:24-25 cautions us ***"But Jesus did not trust Himself to them, because He knew***

The history of socialism suggests that suppressing one economy does not stimulate another, but collapses both. To even advocate enhancing one at the expense of another seems at least covetous, if not an occasion for the sin of theft.

The experience of central bureaucratic planning is one failure after another, on a country-by-country basis. What has not succeeded for autonomous nations would be even more difficult to effect for all the nations of the world, simultaneously. Therefore, it seems reasonable to question the very assumption that 'global consensus' is a desirable goal. Global consensus forgoes the natural evolution of a variety of countries, on their own schedules, and with their own abilities to speed up or slow down, in order to become lock-step with each other, ready or not. Why such lock-step would be desirable is not defended, and may well be indefensible.

There also seems to be an undue emphasis on punishment, penalties, and 'payback,' rather than on incentives and change of heart. An unelected overseer is merely a very old, failed 'solution' to new problems. I hope we will be careful for what we wish. When the people of Israel wanted a ruler over their country instead of God that is exactly what they received, to the ultimate suffering of future generations. I am dismayed by the dragging up of those out-dated, unsuccessful strategies which underpin marxist and socialist nations, rather than learning the lessons of their failures, and concentrating on seeking the fruit of human conversion and productivity; i.e. the Godly path.

When Laudato Si' states:

"International negotiations cannot make significant progress due to positions taken by countries which

place their national interest above the global common good" (#169), this implies that country representatives should be expected to vote against their own national interests, betraying the very responsibilities with which they are reasonably vested. Choosing the lesser betrayal is a poor choice; even a popular end does not justify the means.

It appears that the entire world is targeted in the following words: *"...social ecology is necessarily institutional, and gradually extends to the whole of society...."* (#142)

How can the Catholic social principle of subsidiarity possibly fit with these concepts, if there is denial of free will of the individual, of property rights, of accountability of the elected, and intrusion into the sovereign rights of nations?

Yet, Laudato Si' proposes:

"It is essential to devise stronger and more efficiently organized international institutions, with functionaries who are appointed fairly by agreement among national governments, and empowered to impose sanctions." (#175)

I find myself unable to defend those words as anything except classic socialism. From whence comes the hope that nations, governments and politicians, so roundly criticized for inability (or unwillingness) to act, to rule, to govern and sanction will then appoint (unelected) 'functionaries' in a super-secular and greedy world who will be effective, responsible and above reproach? The entire argument seems to collapse on itself.

Moreover, it is unclear how any of these proposals actually would help the poor, rather than exploit them further.

It is difficult to imagine how appointed 'functionaries' would selectively address such matters, since large collectivist organizations have ultimately no accountability, resulting in being responsible to no one, because they can hide behind being responsible to every one. These are ultimately matters of the individual heart.

Should not the emphasis, rather, be toward conversion of souls rather than promoting a super-sized organizational structure and its impositions? Railing against multinationals hardly seems to create argument for still larger enforcers, whose individual members are as corruptible as anyone else.

As to the accusation of rampant consumerism, would not such "functionaries" also be consumers, like most of the world? Yet Laudato Si' expresses the following concern:

"Obsession with a consumerist lifestyle, above all when few people are capable of maintaining it, can only lead to violence and mutual destruction." (#204)

The threat of class warfare is somewhat implicit in such words. Yet curbing consumerism leads to rationing, which seems to be the proposal, but which almost always has, as its result, creation of a black market. In the United States, Prohibition brought that response to the fore. So did gasoline rationing. Black markets typically suffer the side effect of crime, and further manipulation by those with more financial ability, oversight or power. The ugliest side of 'modifying consumption' comes from the 'sustainability advocates,' who mean fewer people alive and consuming. The Encyclical skirts the issue, supporting the sustainability objective but being silent on the strategy.

There are many strategies for helping the poor other than collectivist approaches, other than suppressing free will. It is concerning that the proposals of Laudato Si' seem very narrow and lacking in creativity, and also stimulating of class struggle. Christ's words in Mark 14:7, *"you always have the poor with you"* show that eliminating poverty is unrealistic.

In summary on this point, the Encyclical seems heavily weighted toward socialistic solutions which are likely to abridge the sovereign rights of nations and, in the extreme, might even echo a call to class warfare, which would be a horrendous division in the Body of Christ.

G. "Who am I to judge?"

Your Holiness will of course recognize the question so often echoed from your return travel after World Youth Day in Brazil. Your words aloft have often been used inaccurately or inappropriately by media and special interest groups. Nevertheless, at its core is a question of judging, and the need for caution in doing so. But there is a certain tone in Laudato Si' which does sound judgmental, and I believe that is unfortunate, as natural human defensiveness then makes any valid message more difficult to absorb and act upon. It is not only a matter of content, but also of tone, and dealing with a translation makes it still more complicated to assess.

There are a number of statements throughout Laudato Si' which seem to ascribe a questionable motive to others, to people, groups or nations. Affluent individuals, multinational companies, and northern-hemisphere countries, in particular, seem to be targeted. The Church and other organized religions substantially escape criticism. There are many direct quotes from Laudato Si', and its frequent proposals of 'money' settlements, which raise questions of motivation. But the point is not regarding any one particular quote, but rather a judgmental tone which ripples throughout the Encyclical.

I will offer only a very few examples of words or phrases directed against those who seem not to be living environmentally as Laudato Si' would dictate. Some terms may well be taken as harsh in tone, even insulting. With a worldwide audience for the Encyclical, it seems a shame to alienate with less than gracious words. For example:

"Obstructionist attitudes" ... *"indifference, nonchalant resignation or blind confidence in technical solutions."* *(#14)*

"...countries ought to help pay this debt by significantly limiting their consumption of non-renewable energy." *(#52)*

"...superficial rhetoric, sporadic acts of philanthropy and perfunctory expressions of concern...." *(#54)*

"...for them maximizing profits is enough." *(#109)*

"...the technological mind sees nature... as raw material to be hammered into useful shape; ...." *(#115)*

"...the last thing either party is concerned about is caring for the environment and protecting those who are most vulnerable." *(#198)*

It is still a mystery to me how the word 'poor' is defined in Laudato Si'. What might be called 'poor' in the United States may be economically well ahead of 'rich' in some other countries. It is also a mystery to me what 'rich' means in Laudato Si', except that it seems to be used negatively, a 4-letter word. The broad-brush indictment of those who are 'rich' does not fit much of what we find in the Bible.

To begin with the Old Testament, Abraham was rich, very rich. So too, therefore, were Isaac and Jacob. Likely also was the little shepherd boy who rose to become the second king of Israel, David, a man after God's 'own heart.' Solomon, exceedingly rich and powerful, even built God's Temple.

In the New Testament, it is true that some who were wealthy were criticized, like the rich man who had the poor man Lazarus at his gate and didn't feed him. But that seems to be an exception, compared to other stories. Christ, the Babe, accepted gold, frankincense and myrrh from pagan kings, likely providing resources for the Flight to Egypt, rather than being immediately given to the poor. Yes, Joseph and Mary were poor, as we see from their offering the turtle doves, but Jesus ate with tax collectors (who tended to be well-to-do), and He recounted the loving father of the prodigal son as a seemingly rich landowner.

Jesus *'loved'* the rich young man (Mark 10:21), even though he did not have the courage to follow Jesus. And it would appear that people from whom Jesus accepted hospitality, like Lazarus of Bethany, were also well off.

In death, Jesus was laid in a rich man's grave, and received the care of both Joseph of Arimathea and Nicodemus, both apparently well-to-do. Jesus did not discriminate against the people God had blessed with 'riches,' and it isn't clear to me why the rich are such specific targets in this Encyclical.

I do not wish to belabor, only to offer a few of the many examples of problematic, even hostile tone. Unfortunately, those excerpts do seem to sound somewhat judgmental. There is a certain sadness or darkness in Laudato Si' that feels to me more alienating than uniting, more depressing than uplifting. Let us all remember the words of Sacred Scripture:

"Therefore encourage one another and build one another up ...." (1 Thessalonians 5:11)

H. Individual action plans have little action

Even if Catholics in the pew were to read through Laudato Si' to assess what more they are being called to do for the environment and ecology, the list is scant. This observation leads to the conclusion that Laudato Si' is written much more in support of worldwide organizational superstructure than for the individual trying to deal with environmental responsibility before the Creator. It is an orientation of 'top down' rather than 'bottom up,' yet true advances in the world almost always have come from the efforts of individuals using their God-given gifts, cooperating with other individuals toward a common goal. It is a shame so little is envisioned and suggested for their action.

Considering that there is no specific claim of infallibility, it is not as if we must ferret out a list of required actions. Rather, the Encyclical seems to be cast more as a justification for bringing in collectivist oversight than in mobilizing a people to action. Perhaps the lack of 'action items' is partly not seeing the matter from the individual's perspective, as might be more the case in, say, pastoral care.

Most of the individual suggestions can be summed up as:

"...[using] less heating and [wearing] warmer clothes... avoiding the use of plastic and paper, reducing water consumption, separating refuse, cooking only what can reasonably be consumed, showing care for other living beings, using public transport or car-pooling, planting trees, turning off unnecessary lights ... reusing something instead of immediately discarding it ... giving thanks to God before and after meals."

In the United States we can contrast the reports of half the nation being on food stamps and the other half's paying for those food stamps, to St. Paul's second letter to the Thessalonians (2 Thessalonians 3:10) in which he writes: ***"If any one will not work, let him not eat."*** Considering the questions raised in Laudato Si' leads one to the conclusion in such complex matters that 'one size does not fit all' when one is striving for solutions, or when striving for the good of souls. Decisions which impact seriously on all the people of the world cannot be taken lightly, or under only the cloak of one person's experience. And this is especially important when one is handing responsibility to mega collectivist organizations instead of adhering to the principle of subsidiarity.

It is good that we have your invitation to dialogue. It also makes sense that similar dialogue should occur among individuals and with local government, to educate and involve people to take care of their communities, to mobilize broader, well-aligned grass-roots efforts, and to brainstorm solutions.

But we also need information. It is difficult to take seriously programs which are proposed or endorsed without revealing the cost, the likely outcomes, and the schedule. What effect will any expensive resource-draining actions have on other needs? How much? And for how long? That these questions can't presently be answered is a good indication of how little is known or can be depended upon from a so-called ecology sector making pronouncements on 'global warming' and 'action plans' across borders.

Unfortunately, the Encyclical itself has an apparent clash between the principle of subsidiarity with actions rising from the bottom up, in which needs and possibilities are generated and implemented by those closest to the problem, and an imposition of top down rules and penalties on a worldwide scale, in a collectivist setting. The two methods inevitably conflict at the point where strategies clash, and then raw power often reigns.

The only truly unsustainable, nonrenewable resource is our own time. To be principally consumed with environmental and ecological matters detracts, in the sense of time and energy, from higher spiritual activities, e.g. worship of God and performing the spiritual and corporal works of mercy. We are creatures, with only 24 hours in a day, and with a single lifetime to know, love and serve God before He calls us home. Unfortunately, Laudato Si' does not give a sense of priority relative to the Greatest Commandment, or to the Great Commission. It seems to stand alone, within its own space, mostly unrelated to (or incompatible with) other responsibilities.

I.   What about the Church's responsibilities?

It is quite disappointing to read: *"Nor are there genuine ethical horizons to which one can appeal." (#110)*

If the Catholic Church is not a "genuine ethical horizon" in her own eyes, then much has been surrendered, and the words of Laudato Si' would have little authority. Moreover, one might see such a concern as not having Faith in the Holy Spirit's protection, to the end of time. The Church must be very careful not to give away the gift entrusted to her, or to give the impression that she has abandoned her patrimonial right to proclaim Christ's Teachings to the world. Due to the presence of the Holy Spirit, the Church does not suffer from that same limitation as large secular infrastructures, which carry the seeds of their own destruction.

The Church should have a unique advantage in being able to work across borders, which governments and secular organizations cannot do as effectively. Instead of transferring power to the United Nations or to collectivist overseers, should not the Church be proclaiming her role to the priorities established by Christ, rather than seeming to impose and settle for behavior modification? Are the ability and willingness to lead being lost?

It is startling to see that so many organizations receive blame in Laudato Si', but not the Catholic Church, her magisterium or even other religions. Everything from the Northern Hemisphere's 'debt' to the Southern Hemisphere's claims, and from people using air-conditioning to multinational companies' financial clout are criticized. But what condemnation is there of the silent pulpit on true life issues?

What about the loss of Catholic schooling, from kindergarten through the university? What about closing churches and alienation of the flock? What about the loss in moral high ground due to the priest sexual-abuse scandal? Is there nothing which the Church and her resources regret or wish had been done differently? How could such silence not have affected the responsiveness to environmental issues now on the table?

If the Church has a legitimate role in concern for the environment, then it is necessary to ask why she has not taken an active leadership role to prevent what is now decried as filth or a garbage dump. If pollution and environmental abuse are indeed the problems which Laudato Si' implies, then what organization more than the Catholic Church would have had the right and obligation to 'teach, govern and sanctify' in these matters?

One would expect an encyclical to stand on that duty, even when not binding infallibly, to articulate what needs to be said as teacher to the world. But when the Catholic Church asserts a collectivist superstructure to be the solution, rather than conversion of souls, she is begging the question of her own authority. When we read: *"Nor are there genuine ethical horizons to which one can appeal,"* what are we to believe about the Church's belief in her own authority? Are not greed, corruption, sloth, and serving mammon instead of God among the many sins which are subject to the Church's judgment, evangelization and teaching?

Perhaps part of the loss in involvement of the individual's activity in the Church is that it mirrors what has happened over the last half century. The tradition of the Church for centuries had been to act on her own to respond to need, i.e. to open monasteries and churches, orphanages, soup kitchens, schools and colleges, hospitals and nursing homes, to provide direct service to those in need. Many of these are now abandoned, and the people served are dispersed to secular organizations, with service replaced by fundraising. Sadly, money has become a 'fungible grace.'

Thus, the mechanism to respond to need is impaired, and the Church more easily cedes her rightful place to government regulation, especially government opposed to Freedom of Religion, as in 1) the closing of Catholic adoption agencies for their lack of willingness to refer to same-sex couples, 2) the reported impairment to veterans' receiving spiritual assistance in veterans' hospitals, 3) termination of chaplains for using the name of Jesus in graveside services, and 4) mandatory insurance for abortion, contraception, sterilization and even transgender surgery! These are not political opinion disputes; they are direct attacks against Christianity and other faiths of similar beliefs, and have already occurred.

Euthanasia is strongly emerging, immoral and anti-Christian, but legal in an increasing number of nations for heirs to dispatch parents, parents to eliminate young children. Mark 13:12 foresees both abortion and euthanasia as signs of the end times. Elective euthanasia is the sin from which there is little opportunity for repentance. There also are virtually no Catholic sanctuaries to which to escape political forces, and hardly any strong preaching from which a Catholic might identify a priest who fully supports Church Teaching. Yet the gated communities, overwatered golf courses and inadequate recycling are subjects of an Encyclical. I mean this comment not to criticize, but to transmit the cry of souls who now, more than ever, need strong and committed Church Teaching, not splitting hairs or offering politically correct arguments, and not commonality of concerns with the world. Our home is not here. Our true 'common home' lies in the next life.

As the Church has become more of a 'middleman distributor' of financial resources to other organizations, which often function outside of the Church's direct control, the link of the Faithful to the work itself is seriously weakened and unfocused. Recipient organizations sometimes flout Catholic Teaching in the way they disburse funds and so scandalize souls. Thus there is a pyramid, with decreasing control, that funds what the Church can't even track as provider. It is not surprising, then, when the Faithful reasonably determine that they can distribute their own financial resources better than the United States Conference of Catholic Bishops, its allied organizations and recipients around the world.

Excerpted quotes from Laudato Si', with some frequency, involve finances or power or both (even in *"A Christian Prayer in Unity with Creation"* in Chapter XV!) But there is very little mentioned regarding the Church's key mission to encourage hearts to change. Rather, there is more emphasis in this Encyclical on behavior modification than on spiritual metanoia.

It would be difficult, even for the heroic saints of old, to arise from these ashes of abandoned servanthood, rather than merely facilitating its fundraising. Certainly it is reasonable for us to look to the words of Jesus in determining what is important, and what is not. We want to inherit the world which He promised to make new, but we should have no illusions that we are being asked to do the reconstruction ourselves!

Where is the Church herself to be found — in the battle for souls or in an environmental skirmish? If the Church cannot teach what is necessary in ethics and morals, who can? An intriguing comment in Laudato Si' is raised by the words:

"An inadequate presentation of Christian anthropology gave rise to a wrong understanding of the relationship between human beings and the world." (#116)

One must ask: "An inadequate presentation by whom? And how will it be rectified?" This is one of the few references that may recognize that at least part of the current trauma is from poor catechesis.

And that, in turn, reminds us of Christ's question to His listeners: ***"... nevertheless, when the Son of Man comes, will He find faith on earth?"*** (Luke 18:8)

J. Environmental education, other concerns

Chapter #6 in Laudato Si' is entitled "Ecological Education and Spirituality," which makes me quite uncomfortable. One reason is that these items of faith are separated from, rather than woven through, the entire Encyclical. If integral to the text, it would strengthen every section with what the Church teaches and we believe to be truth. We are warned in Mark 8:38 and Luke 9:26 that we must not be ashamed of His Word. We must be careful, I believe, not to compartmentalize God and His Teachings, as they are ***'all in all'*** (Ephesians 1:23), and nothing matters except in His context.

A second reason for discomfort is that the titles of the subsections tend not to be as one would expect religious teaching to be organized, witnessing to fundamental doctrine; rather, we see titles like "The Trinity and the Relationship between Creatures," and "Sacramental Signs and Celebration of Rest," and "Beyond the Sun." There is too little detail to adequately respond with analysis, but the discomfort persists about what the ultimate purpose is for these sections, how they will be used, and what is the risk of embedding syncretism.

A third reason for some discomfort is a selection of isolated sentences about environmental education in particular. All education is the right and prerogative of the parents, but it is not clear what the implications are for these statements on environmental education. They may show up some time in the future, with a different meaning than I am now able to comprehend. Sentences in this section could provoke a discourse in their own right, so it seems presumptuous to try to analyze the intended meaning in just a few pages.

I cannot definitively say what the full meaning of the environmental education quotations might be, or whether or not they fit in with a socialistic approach to education. Some of the following quotes seem to show echoes of cultic or mind-forming activity in the education process, although they may have originally been used in an entirely different context:

"Environmental education has broadened its goals ... it tends now to include a critique of the 'myths' of a modernity grounded in a utilitarian mindset (individualism, unlimited progress, competition, consumerism, the unregulated market)." (#210)

"Environmental education should facilitate ... through effective pedagogy, to grow in solidarity, responsibility and compassionate care." (#210)

"Yet this education [is] aimed at creating an 'ecological citizenship,' ...." (#211)

"The work of dominating the world calls for a union of skills and a unity of achievement that can only grow from quite a different attitude." (#219) Dominating the world? Who? Why?

"...we need institutions empowered to impose penalties for damage inflicted on the environment ...." (#214)

"Our efforts at education will be inadequate and ineffectual unless we strive to promote a new way of thinking about human beings, life, society and our relationship with nature. (#215)

"...community actions, when they express self-giving love, can ... become intense spiritual experiences." (#232)

"The majority of the members of society must be adequately motivated ... personally transformed to respond." (#211)

The fourth reason for some discomfort rests in two prayers introduced in Laudato Si'. They are quite different from the classic prayers of the Catholic Faith, of which the Canticle of Daniel is perhaps the best known prayer of nature, frequently used in the Liturgy of the Hours, offering intense praise to God 'by' all of His Creation.

But the prayers Laudato Si' offers are not spoken by creation toward God, but by our praying 'for' creation. There are also words which sound accusatory toward those who don't quite agree that the causes of current environmental issues are simply attributable to a 'rich-vs.-poor' class struggle. There is a discomfort in that the prayers do not sound like the way we usually pray for others.

The following two intercessions are put forth in Laudato Si':

"Touch the hearts of those who look only for gain at the expense of the poor and the earth." (#246)

"Enlighten those who possess power and money that they may avoid the sin of indifference, that they may love the common good, advance the weak, and care for this world in which we live." (#246)

I can not say definitively that there is anything wrong about the prayers; however, I can say I find accusatory targeting of the rich and the powerful to be inappropriate and ineffective, and I can't imagine myself ever offering up such an intercession at Mass in the wording of either prayer. I can't imagine myself even silently praying such a prayer.

It is unfortunate and unnecessary, I believe, to allow those kinds of division to enter into the Church. Yet, that is what the 'new prayers' seem to do, which I find of concern.

Final thoughts

Your Holiness, I do contrast the work of Laudato Si' with some of the great and pressing needs of the Church and of the world. Just as I have expressed concern about taking the time and effort of people to fight on an environmental front with their limited resources, on matters still unproven, so too I am concerned that the writing, publishing and teaching of Laudato Si' will detract from much more urgent and important elements of Christ's message and the Church's real priorities.

It would be less than honest, after all this dialogue, not to note that I have searched both the Encyclical and the New Testament to try to find any precedent for special care of the environment as put forth in Laudato Si', and the evidence is sparse. Yes, Christ calmed the storms but he didn't command us to do so; or to try to manage the weather. Rather, He made it a matter of Faith. He expected Nicodemus to be able to observe and understand the weather, God's prerogative.

Christ did ask the woman at the well for water (John 4) and also commended those who give the thirsty a ***"cup of water"*** in His Name (Mark 9:41). Addressing water poverty issues is indeed relevant. Nevertheless, where can one find broader environmental and ecological issues referenced in the Bible? Perhaps the lack of such references in Laudato Si' is one indication that we don't have relevant sources?

Holy Father, I can only hope and pray that the Holy Spirit will always direct your work, strengthen your flock for what may well be the end-times, to not give up on the teachings of the Gospels at this late date, to not allow re-inventing of the Faith, but to hold firm to what we have been taught.

§§§§§§ *A Story* §§§§§§

I offer one closing thought regarding a Church in crisis. It is a story from wartime Poland recounted by an enthusiastic tour guide giving part of the 'Walking in the Footsteps of Pope John Paul II' tour. It is a story worth repeating since it well represents the soul of the flock which so badly needs a shepherd's presence and guidance. It is also an apt metaphor for today's times.

During World War II, as a result of shelling, much of a roof had been blown off a Catholic Church. All the priests who had been serving in the area had been sent to death camps. Yet the Catholics of the parish community gathered in the ruins of the Church on Sunday mornings, even when the rain was pouring through the almost roofless ceiling, even when it was bitterly cold. They would first go to the sacristy and find the proper colored vestments for that Sunday, and lay them gently and reverently on the altar, alongside the vessels of celebration. Then they would recite the prayers of the Mass as best they were able, and they wept. Of course there was no Eucharist, but their hearts were united to Christ. And their cry for a priest must have risen like a profound oblation.

I suggest that our Church today may be in a bit of a similar situation. Over the past half century, the roof to some extent has been blown off by scandals within and by persecution from outside. We are at the mercy of many elements, especially those most secular. Not all our priests are or have been faithful, as empty vestments testify. Yet we worship and pray for relief. We pursue our faith and let it pursue us. And when a true shepherd of souls fills the vestments, we follow, because we will always recognize His voice.

We remember especially the words of St. Paul to the Galatians 1:8: ***"But even if we, or an angel from heaven, should preach to you a gospel contrary to that which we preached to you, let him be accursed."*** Thank you, Holy Father, for your invitation for dialogue. I am grateful for the opportunity to offer this **"Half a Dialogue"** to you, and hope it will create some value in honor of the Lord.

Respectfully submitted in Christ,

Diane C. Harris

Appendices

Appendix A

COMMENTARY

One scientist's take on global warming

My top 10 reasons for cooling on global warming:

10) Being a scientist by training means not accepting anything without as much proof as required to reject it. There is no proof there is global warming, or that there is not global warming. Therefore, a true scientist keeps an open mind. (Not believing is not the same as disbelieving.) Until there is irrefutable proof, there is no reason to make a decision, either way.

9) Irrefutable proof is unlikely. The scientific method requires observation of multiple phenomena, developing alternative theories, designing experiments to test hypotheses. There are too few years (data points) available even to hypothesize global warming, let alone to test possible causes. Without a controlled laboratory environment, there is no way to separate variables and make statistical quality observations to "prove" or to "disprove" global warming theory.

8) Sophisticated instrumentation and data

DIANE HARRIS

gathering is less than a century old. Not enough time has elapsed to record natural cycles of warm and cold weather to determine inherent variability (baseline) against which to examine changes.

7) Scientists should champion truth, not poll what is true or not. Truth cannot be subjected to a survey. Even if every scientist in the world believes in global warming, it would not be "proof." Truth is truth even when no one believes it; error is error even when everyone believes it.

6) The very presence of a "consensus" argument (e.g. "everybody KNOWS there is global warming") undermines its credibility as a scientific conclusion. Real scientists don't use consensus arguments; they use data and proof,

not anecdotal polar bears on an iceberg, however manipulatively sad.

5) Follow the money. Scientists are human beings, and most do not reject government funding, prestige, grants or awards upon which their livelihoods depend. It is unlikely much grant money will be available to disprove global warming. Thus, the deck is stacked with funding for scientists willing to write grant proposals to prove global warming or to ameliorate its theoretical impact, not to disprove it.

4) If the U.S. government really believes global warming is caused by environmental pollution, coal gases or myriad alleged related causes, imports should be banned from countries with inferior pollution standards, and more controllable domestic manufacturing encouraged. Why is such reasonable response, with job creation, not implemented?

3) The "global warming industry" has long-term sustainability as a business sector. It has no "endpoint"

like a Salk vaccine. How will we know when we've been successful? We won't. Global warming employment is a "renewable" non-productive job opportunity ad infinitum, with each failure becoming an impetus for more government funding, and associated higher taxes.

2) In a public square where freedom to sin is protected (but not preaching against it), a militaristic-style onslaught against the imagined enemy of global warming has the potential to become a state religion, suppressing heretics who believe false gods of global warming are not to be appeased, but uniting in choir those who do.

1) If, indeed, there were any real global warming, then many explanations are being completely ignored. Maybe we're just getting closer to hell?

Diane Harris lives in Middlesex, has a master's degree in chemistry from Rensselaer Polytechnic Institute and is a retired vice president of Bausch and Lomb.

Published in the Canandaigua Daily Messenger, May 8, 2014

Appendix B
<u>Kalama Water Poverty Project</u>

In Laudato Si', Pope Francis writes a riveting phrase: "Water Poverty." Moreover, he mentions water 47x in the text, stating strongly: *"Our world has a grave social debt towards the poor who lack access to drinking water, because they are denied the right to a life consistent with their inalienable dignity." (#30)*

How could anyone deny the fundamental human right to water? Yet, how is this need to be satisfied? The dilemma for many people, who may be sensitive and responsive to the water poverty issue, is "What can we do about it?" To reduce our own consumption of water has little direct effect on those in more deprived areas of the world. Moreover, adequate consumption of water is essential to human health; 'fasting' from water, even in a spirit of sacrifice, may be an inappropriate risk, insufficiently respectful of caring for the bodies God has given us. But 'shipping water over water' (i.e. by ship or by plane across an ocean) is impracticable due to cost.

Some might imagine, on a grand and strategic scale of problem solving, that small communities (even in more affluent areas) lack the ability to solve 'water poverty' thousands of miles away. But one parish has shown, when led in conscience and formed with commitment, that it is possible to make a real and significant difference. God is indeed always present to bless dreams that are in His Will.

The problems associated with responding to water need in a remote area of the globe were successfully addressed by the Kalama Project, which serves as an excellent model for many parishes and other organizations to address such need without mega resources. Here's what happened:

Talking / Listening / Praying / Acting

In 2009, a priest from Kalama, a small village in Kenya, was studying in the U.S. for his undergraduate and Masters degrees in biology and simultaneously serving in a parish consisting of approximately 2500 families. One day the deacon asked him about the needs of the village from which he had come, and Father Dominic mentioned water as the pre-eminent need of his entire village.

"Water is life," said Father Dominic

The parish in which he was serving at the time is in a region of Western New York State with incredible blessing of potable and abundant recreational water supplies. Thus, there was a daily reminder of how much natural blessing there is in some areas, while other parts of the world thirst. Father Dominic told his story of walking miles to and from a polluted river with the other children, before and after school, to eke out barely enough water for survival of the people, a few animals, and small garden crops. Father Dominic recalled how difficult that made it to have enough time to study, and how the economic situation in Kalama (most people earn less than $150 per year) made it impossible to send the children to high school or college. That resulted in no local access to routine medical care and treatment, both because of the water situation and because of lack of education to acquire necessary skills.

After much dialogue, prayer and building of true relationship in Christ, the Kalama project was launched as a mutual effort between the people of Kalama and the people from the parish of about 2500 families, characterized from the very beginning by a mutual deep human respect and caring, not as a disembodied charity work, but as a flowing together of hearts across an ocean.

<u>**A Well for Kalama**</u>

It was mutually determined between the parish and the people of Kalama that the greatest need was for a bored water well and the ability to run and maintain it, with an estimated cost of approximately $65,000. What could not have been anticipated was the extraordinary blessing on that project, as the resultant bored well tested as being "the second most successful borehole project in Kenya." The volume of water exceeded expectations so dramatically that a forty foot tower was erected so that water could be stored in a tank atop the tower then fed by gravity to the more remote portions of the area. Then funds were provided for an additional pipeline; the villagers dug the trenches and laid the pipe by hand.

The well was dug in the summer of 2010, and is 450 feet (160 meters) deep, with excellent flow, and was drilled at a cost of about $40,000. Some of the pumps and supplies were donated. Staff was trained to care for the water supply and to protect it. The people of Kalama did almost all the on-site work and also extended the initial flow to additional distribution points. With the friendship that had been formed, hearts were open to looking at other needs as well, made possible by the presence of potable water. This first phase meant that the children no longer had to walk 15 minutes before climbing down a cliff to reach the Athi River, where they could gather contaminated water for washing, and for kitchen crops (but not for human consumption.)

<u>**Water opens a door**</u>

The water enabled so much more to be accomplished in the Kalama Community. Since 2009, over $100,000 has been raised, through larger and smaller donations, even from the children's 'trick or treating' for 'Coins for Kalama' in the United States. In addition to the water well, educational scholarships were established. Three students were sponsored for high school education, one student has been trained as a teacher, another student is completing a clinical medicine diploma, one is sponsored for a BSA in nursing and Public Health, and a new student is being sponsored in medical school to pursue a degree in medicine and surgery. As these students receive their degrees and return to the Kalama community, their presence will elevate the level of health and well-being.

A medical clinic has been constructed, and medical equipment and medicines donated. A nursery school was established to minimize some of the long distance walking for the young children. Approximately $10,000 per year, raised by the parish faith community, is needed to maintain stability in the current situation, and the project team has been successful each year in doing so. The people of Kalama continue to do as much of the work themselves as possible. The Kalama Project was not simply a one-time response to a particular need, but forming of a deep relationship and commitment.

The mystery of how 'Water Poverty' can be alleviated by people an ocean away was solved. The model is adaptable to other faith communities, and does not require a 'mega-church' to do so.

It isn't about water; it is about people

While all of these associated projects undertaken have been blessed with remarkable success, it is truly more about the building of deep relationships and trust between the communities, and having a person "on the ground" (Father Dominic) who is an excellent steward for both communities. The relationship is also supported by visits from young adults in the parish community on a regular basis, not paid for through the donations to the Kalama project, but through their own efforts and desire to participate. For those involved in either geographical area, there is no doubt that they have family, just an ocean away.

Information and donations

For information on how to begin such a project or how to contribute to such a project, contact the Diocese of Machakos:

The Kalama Project
Diocese of Machakos
c/o Bishop's Residence
P.O. Box 344
90100 Machakos, Kenya
Telephone (044)21.554 or fax: 21.308

References:

http://www.catholiccourier.com/regional-life/yatesontariowayne/features/kalama-project-puts-faith-into-action/

http://www.kalamaproject.com/8cnuy5xdlj9pcjd1433csf196yynb5

http://www.kalamaproject.com/5k4k/

http://www.grtconline.org/calendar/79-5k/125-5k-for-kalama

http://www.stbenedictonline.org/service/kalama/

Note: This Appendix B regarding the Kalama Project in Kenya spotlights what is possible in the challenge of water poverty, and invites participation. It is not an endorsement of the contents of the monograph "Half a Dialogue" by anyone associated with the Kalama Project. It is not a representation on behalf of the Kalama Project by the author or publisher of "Half a Dialogue."

Appendix C

<u>Suggested Reading on 'Global Warming' and Alleged 'Climate Change'</u>

Note: these are not claimed as reference books for **"Half a Dialogue."** Rather, for anyone willing to take the scientific issue seriously, these materials are suggested reading for forming a more balanced opinion in a world that is covering its ears to anything which disputes the approved public opinion. In effect, true science is suffering at the tongues of consensual bullies.

<u>A Disgrace to the Profession</u>, Volume I, Compiled and Edited by Mark Steyn, 2015, Stockade Publishing LLC, Woodsville, NH 03785.
"The World's Scientists — in their own words — on Michael Mann, his hockey stick, and the damage to Science."

<u>The Whole Story of Climate: What Science Reveals About the Nature of Endless Change</u>, by Dr. E. Kirsten Peters, 2012, Prometheus Books, Amherst, NY 14228
"Writing anything at all about climate is complex, and is almost bound to be controversial."

<u>Global Warming Alarmists, Skeptics and Deniers</u>, A Geoscientist Looks at the Science of Climate, by G. Dedrick Robinson, 2012, Moonshine Cove Publishing LLC, Abbeville, SC 29620
"'It is a capital mistake to theorize before one has data. Unintentionally one begins to twist facts to suit theories, instead of theories to fit facts.' Sherlock Holmes in Sir Arthur Conan Doyle's <u>A Scandal in Bohemia</u>, 1891."

The Deliberate Corruption of Climate Science, by Tim Ball, PhD., 2014, Stairway Press, Mount Vernon, WA 98273.
"It ... undermined the environmental movement by incorrectly claiming massive environmental damage and setting up a classic 'cry wolf' scenario."

The Inconvenient Skeptic: the Comprehensive Guide to the Earth's Climate, by John H, Kehr, 2011, John Kehr Publisher.
"There is no time to waste on bad ideas, so I am used to quickly discarding [them]. In my view it is time to discard the theory of Anthropogenic Global Warming (AGW)."

Climate Change: the Facts, Edited by Alan Moran, 2015, Institute of Public Affairs, Melbourne, Victoria, Australia.
"Prompted by successive reports of the Intergovernmental Panel on Climate Change (IPCC), the issue of human induced climate change has become a dominant theme of world politics."

The Climate Fix; What Scientists and Politicians Won't Tell You About ..., by Roger Pielke, Jr., 2010, Basic Books, A Member of the Perseus Books Group, New York
"For some, the climate debate is a morality play, with good guys and bad guys, with virtue and reason on one side and evil and corruption on the other."

The Greatest Hoax: How the Global Warming Conspiracy Threatens ..., by U.S. Senator James Inhofe, 2012, WND Books, Washington, DC
"...Time Magazine ... in 1974 told us that another ice age was coming and we were all going to die."

Appendix D
<u>Word Index for Laudato Si'</u>

Words are listed by paragraph number with more than one occurrence in any paragraph indicated by that number in parentheses ( ); footnotes are bracketed [ ].

- Abortion: 120
- Agriculture / Agricultural: 4, 21, 23, 24, 25, 28 (2), 34, 41, 51, 125, 129 (2), 131, 133, 146, 1647, 180 (3)
- Air-conditioning: 55
- Biodiverse(ity): 24, 32, 35, 37, 38(2), 39(2), 167, 169, 190, 195
- Carbon dioxide: 23, 24(2), 26, 140
- Catechism: 69, 86, 130(2), [37], [41], [42], [49] (2), [63], [69], [106], [107], [108], [168]
- Catholic: 3, 7, 63, 130, [22], [25], [31], [37], [3], [49], [55], [56], [63], [69], [78], [106], [153], [168]
- Change(s), (d): 4, 5, 8, 9, 13(2), 15, 18(4), 20, 23(2), 24(2), 25(3), 26, 46, 52, 54, 60, 61, 102, 113, 139, 151, 161, 163, 169, 170, 171, 172, 181(2), 184, 194, 197, 202(2), 2069, 208, 209, 211, 212, 215, 217, 218(2), 219, [31]
- Christ: 83 (3), 98, 99 (3), 121, 217, 221, 235
- Christian(s): 7, 9, 10, 15, 64 (2), 65, 67, 93, 98, 99, 116, 119, 125, 214, 216 (3), 217 (2), 221, 222 (2), 235 (2), 237, 239, 246 (2)
- Christianity: 121, 235
- Church('s), (es): 3, 7(3), 15, 61, 63(2), 67, 69, 79, 93, 130, 131, 175, 188, 214, 216, 231, 235, 236, 242, [28], [37], [41], [43], [49], [50], [63], [69], [86], [100], [106], [118], [1522], [131], [134], [158], [168]
- City(ies): 21, 28, 44(3), 49, 126, 143(2), 149, 150, 151(3), 152(3), 153(3), 154, 192, [128]
- Climate change: 20, 24 (2), 25 (2), 26, 52, 169, 170, 172, 181, [31]

Appendix E
<u>List of References</u>

1. <u>The Holy Bible</u>, Revised Standard Version Catholic Edition; Old Testament Section, 1952, New Testament Section, 1946; Oxford University Press, Oxford; *Nihil Obstat* Thomas Hanlon, S.T.L.,L.S.S., PH.L.; *Imprimatur Cardinal Gordon Joseph, Archbishop of Saint Andrews and Edinburgh, Feast of Epiphany 1996.*

2. <u>Code of Canon Law,</u> Latin - English Edition. Canon Law Society of America, 1983.

3. The Holy Father, Pope Francis; Laudato Si' an *Encyclical Letter on Care for our Common Home, given in Rome, June* 2015; Libreria Editrice Vaticana.

4. Ratzinger, Joseph Cardinal; <u>Instruction on Certain Aspects of the "Theology of Liberation"</u> on August 6, 1984, approved at an audience granted to the Cardinal Prefect by his Holiness Pope John Paul II, who ordered its publication. Given at Rome, at the Sacred Congregation for the Doctrine of the Faith, on August 6, 1984, the Feast of the Transfiguration of Our Lord.

5. Pope St. John Paul II; <u>Fides et Ratio</u>, an Encyclical to the Bishops of the Catholic Church on the Relationship between Faith and Reason; given in Rome, September 14, 1998, Libreria Editrice Vaticana.

6. On the Trail of Aparecida:
www.americamagazine.org/trail-aparecida

7. <u>Catechism of the Catholic Church</u>. Second Edition, Doubleday, a division of Random House Publishing, 1995.

8. Ratzinger, Joseph Cardinal with Vittori Messori, <u>The Ratzinger Report An Exclusive Interview on the State of the Church.</u> Ignatius Press, San Francisco, 1985.

9. Pope Benedict XVI, <u>Caritas in Veritate,</u> an Encyclical Letter on Integral Human Development in Charity and

Truth, given in Rome, June 29, 2009; Libreria Editrice Vaticana.

10. Pope Benedict XVI, Address to United Nations General Assembly, April 18, 2008.

11. Pope John Paul II, <u>Ordinatio Sacerdotalis</u>, an Apostolic Letter to the Bishops of the Catholic Church on Reserving Priestly Ordination to Men Alone; given in Rome, May 22, 1994, Libreria Editrice Vaticana.

12. Hitchcock, Dr. James, <u>History of the Catholic Church from the Apostolic Age to the Third Millennium</u>; Ignatius Press, San Francisco, 2012.

13. <u>The Divine Office, the Liturgy of the Hours according to the Roman Rite.</u> Harper Collins Publishers, 1975.

14. <u>V General Conference of the Bishops of Latin America and the Caribbean, Concluding Document</u>, Aparecida, May 13-31, 2007, Consejo Episcopal LatinoAmericano, CELAM, June 2008.

15. Mosher, Steven W., <u>Population Research Institute Review.</u> Vol. 26, Number 1, Jan-Feb 2016 "Out of Africa Comes a Cry for Help Against the Culture of Death."

Appendix F

On-line Sources for News References

A number of references in "**Half a Dialogue**" are news stories on-line, available through URL links. Those stories are listed below by major subject area, and then in chronological order. Generally, it would be inconvenient for most readers to try to manually and painstakingly type URL links from text into their own browsers. Therefore, the source material in Appendix F is identified below, and the specific links can be found on the website www.HypotPublishing.com for direct access under the tab: "**About Half a Dialogue.**" See also Cleansing Fire blogsite: www.CleansingFire.org

Relevant Links
(active 3/7/2016)

GENERAL AND CHURCH-RELATED LINKS:

1. **The Liturgy of the Hours:** www.Universalis.com

2. **Homily of Pope Paul VI;** Mass on the 9th Anniversary of the Crowning of His Holiness Paul VI on the Solemnity of the Apostles Peter and Paul, Vatican, June 29, 1972.

3. **Pope John Paul II's Encyclical Letter "Fides et Ratio;"** September 9, 1998.

4. Pope Bendict XVI's Encyclical Letter "Caritas in Veritate;" Vatican, June 29, 2009.

5. On the Trail of Aparecida: Jorge Bergoglio and the Latin American Ecclesial Tradition; American Magazine; October 30, 2013; by Ernesto Cavassa, Jr.

6. Leader of Catholic-Funded Org. Performs Same-Sex Marriages; Lepanto Institute; January 13, 2015; by Michael Hichborn, President.

7. A Christian Prayer in Unity with Creation; Pope Francis' Encyclical Letter Laudato Si', paragraph #246, May 24, 2015.

8. Meet the Muslim Mystic Pope Francis Cited in His Encyclical; TIME Magazine, June 18, 2015; by Aisha Bhoori.

9. Technological Singularity; Wikipedia, November 1, 2015.

ABORTION / STERILIZATION LINKS:

1. UN Official to Vatican: Catholic Teaching on Abortion May be a Form of Torture; LifeSite News (Geneva, Switzerland); May 5, 2014; by Ben Johnson.

2. A 'Mass Sterilization' exercise: Kenyan doctors find anti-fertility agent in UN tetanus vaccine; LifeSite News; November 6, 2014; by Steve Weatherbe.

3. **Kenyan Government launches probe into claim UN is using vaccines for 'mass sterilization';** LifeSite News; November 12, 2014; by Steve Weatherbe.

4. **UN Denies secretly sterilizing Kenyan Women: More Hard Tests Coming;** LifeSite News; November 14, 2014; by Steve Weatherbe.

5. **The UN and the Vatican: Politicizing Torture to Defend Abortion;** Patheos; May 7, 2015; by Rebecca Hamilton.

6. **Boycott Polio Vaccine over Safety Concerns Kenyan Bishops Urge Faithful;** LifeSite News; August 3, 2015; by Lisa Bourne.

7. **CCHD gives $65,000 to group led by donor to pro-abortion and same-sex marriage causes;** Church Militant; August 12, 2015; by Michael Hichborn, President, Lepanto Institute.

8. **The Pope's Unforgiving Message of Forgiveness on Abortion;** New York Times; September 10, 2015; by Jill Filipovic.

9. **200+ congressmen back elderly nuns against 'oppressive' abortifacient HHS mandate;** LifeSite News; January 11, 2016; by Dustin Siggins.

EUTHANASIA LINKS

1. In Belgium, 18% of patients who die are killed by their doctors"; LifeSite News; March 18, 2015; by Wesley J. Smith.

2. Almost 1000 deaths are hastened without explicit request each year in Belgium; LifeSite News; March 19, 2015; by Alex Schadenberg.

3. Almost half of the Belgian euthanasia deaths may not have been reported in 2013; LifeSite News; March 24, 2015; by Alex Schadenberg.

4. Québec doctors' survey shows that the euthanasia law will be abused; LifeSite News; April 27, 2015; by Alex Schadenberg.

5. Dutch pediatricians: Allow euthanasia for children under 12; LifeSite News; June 22, 2015; by Thaddeus Baklinski.

6. Healthy 24-year-old woman to be euthanized in Belgium; LifeSite News; June 23, 2015; by Alex Schadenberg.

7. Surely you're joking, Mr. Denton – Belgian euthanasia is a problem free zone?; LifeSite News; November 5, 2015; by Tom Mortier,

8. There's never enough death for euthanasia fanatics; LifeSite News (The Netherlands); November 15, 2015; by Wesley J. Smith.

9. The underground Dutch system for do-it-yourself euthanasia; LifeSite News; December 1, 2015; by Michael Cook.

10. The coming euthanasia bureaucracy; LifeSite News; December 14, 2015; by Wesley J. Smith.

11. The Netherlands approves euthanasia for severe dementia; LifeSite News; January 8, 2016; by Alex Schadenberg.

12. Keeping the piranhas busy: the terrifying implications of legalizing assisted suicide; LifeSite News; January 27, 2016; by Jonathon Van Maren.

13. Ontario ratifies policy forcing doctors to take part in euthanizing patients; LifeSite News; January 27, 2016; by Steve Weatherbe.

RELIGIOUS PERSECUTION LINKS

1. Veterans banned from saying 'God' or 'Jesus' at military funerals; Daily Mail (UK); June 3, 2011; by John Stevens.

2. Catholic Physicians who want to follow their consciences must emigrate UK expert says; LifeSite News (London); May 3, 2014; by Hilary Whitney.

3. VA Hospital takes down Veteran's Christmas Decorations; (Video) USA Today (reported on KENS-

TV5 , San Antonio, TX); December 13, 2015; by Jeremy Baker.

4. US Army Chaplain reprimanded for citing Scripture in suicide prevention program; LifeSite News; December 18, 2014; by Lisa Bourne.

5. Boston doctor loses final appeal after he was fired for opposing hospital's LGBT agenda; LifeSite News; December 21, 2015; by Mass Resistance.

6. Oregon bakery pays damages in lesbian wedding cake case; Reuters; December 29, 2015; by Shelby Sebens.

<u>U.N. AND SUSTAINABILITY LINKS</u>

1. Earth Charter website; Earth Charter in Action.

2. Report of the UN Conference on Environment and Development; United Nations, Rio Conference; June 3 — June 14, 1992.

3. Financing the UN's Sustainable Development Goals; Forbes Magazine; June 29, 2009; by Ashoka.

4. SD2015; Sustainable Development 2015.

5. Know the Sustainable Development Goals: First end Poverty; Greenbiz; July 21, 2015; by Karin Laljani and Mike Tuffrey.